IMAGES
of America

MARTIN'S AND MILLER'S
GREENSBORO

This view, on South Elm Street looking north, was taken from the Guilford Building *c.* 1950.

IMAGES
of America

MARTIN'S AND MILLER'S
GREENSBORO

J. Stephen Catlett

ARCADIA
PUBLISHING

Published by Arcadia Publishing
Charleston, South Carolina

For all general information contact Arcadia Publishing at:
Telephone 843-853-2070
Fax 843-853-0044
E-mail sales@arcadiapublishing.com
For customer service and orders:
Toll-Free 1-888-313-2665

Visit us on the Internet at www.arcadiapublishing.com

Malcolm A. Miller and
Carol W. Martin pose in
1946, the first year of their
business partnership.

CONTENTS

Acknowledgments   6

Introduction   7

1.   Martin and Miller   9

2.   Photojournalism   17

3.   Around Town   29

4.   Now and Then   41

5.   School Life   55

6.   Children   67

7.   Faces   77

8.   Sports   91

9.   Entertainment and Leisure   105

10.   Business and Industry   119

ACKNOWLEDGMENTS

This book would not have been possible without the assistance and encouragement of many people. I want to thank the Martin family, especially Carol's wife, Ruth, and son, Jim, both of whom have been very encouraging and helpful to me over the past few years. I feel very fortunate to have been able to meet and get to know Carol, and his death in July 1993 was a major loss for everyone. Fortunately, Malcolm Miller is still going strong and has been very supportive of my efforts. He has been most willing to answer any questions I had, no matter how obscure or trivial they sometimes must have seemed. I will always consider it a career highlight to have had the privilege of knowing these two creative, hard working, quintessential professionals.

There are many others who deserve thanks. It is always nice, helpful, and makes for a better product when you have someone to bounce ideas off of, and archives assistant Francis D. "Jim" Pitts has been very receptive and willing to give me his very thoughtful and creative opinions. My volunteers have been no less helpful. T. Edgar Sikes Jr., Joe Melvin, Dick Claycomb, and the late Dick Waggoner have re-foldered and labeled thousands of negatives since 1994 and have called my attention to many interesting images I would have otherwise missed. They have also given a bit of life to the museum archives and made it a more enjoyable place to work. The Weaver Center Intern Program, sponsored by the Guilford County Schools and the City of Greensboro, has provided many energetic high school students over the years, many having worked with the Martin's collection, including the following: Selena Staley (Northwest, 1994), Jason Kovarik (Grimsley, 1996), Jennifer Burnett (Page, 1997), Elizabeth Hannaum (Page, 1998), and Dana Loggins (Northwest, 1999). I thank each of you for your contributions and for constantly reminding me that, contrary to popular opinion, the younger generation is doing quite well indeed.

I want to thank my colleagues at the Museum—Director Bill Moore, Gayle Fripp, Linda Evans, Don Henderson, Betty Montgomery, Shawna Populorum (who left this year), Shirley Sumner, and Susan Webster—for their encouragement, support, and assistance, without which the Martin's exhibit and book would have never been finished.

And lastly, a special thanks to my wife, Leslie, son Evan, and daughter Jean-Marie, for supporting my enthusiasm for the Martin's images, many copies of which I brought home looking to see if, in other's eyes, they were as great as I thought they were.

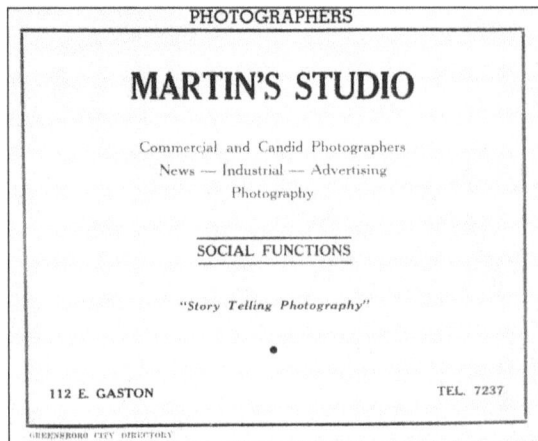

PHOTOGRAPHERS

MARTIN'S STUDIO

Commercial and Candid Photographers
News — Industrial — Advertising
Photography

SOCIAL FUNCTIONS

"Story Telling Photography"

•

112 E. GASTON   TEL. 7237

GREENSBORO CITY DIRECTORY

This was Martin's first City Directory advertisement, which appeared in the 1947–1948 book.

INTRODUCTION

Soon after I came to the museum in 1986, I went down the street to Martin's Studio to take some photographs to be copied for an exhibit. That was the first time I met Carol Martin and Malcolm Miller. Over the next few years, I visited periodically with them, always lingering longer than I should have, always fascinated at Carol's descriptions of some bit of Greensboro history he had seen up close or to hear him talk about the real story behind one of his photographs. Malcolm always seemed to be hovering busily but quietly in the background, working on orders but breaking in when appropriate or if asked to help straighten out any wavering facts. It was an atmosphere I always looked forward to experiencing again and which I have missed tremendously since their studio closed in 1992.

This book is the outgrowth of an exhibit that the author has been working on for many years and that will open at the Greensboro Historical Museum in January 2000. I began thinking about an exhibit from that first hot day in June 1992, when my son and I moved some 250 boxes of negatives, in stifling heat, the one block from Martin's Studio to the museum. A few peeks at some of the 200,000 negatives we were carrying brought great excitement, as I realized that each drop of perspiration was falling on boxes that held a treasure of local visual history that could never be matched in my lifetime.

When deciding how best to organize this book, I realized that it would be easiest just to follow the ten areas around which I had organized the exhibit: Studio/Biographical history, Photojournalism, Around Town, Now & Then, Children, School Life, Faces, Sports, Entertainment and Leisure, and Business. Although the images in this book span the period from the late 1930s until the 1970s this is not, nor is the exhibit itself, a narrative history of Greensboro during these years. Although vast in quantity and scope, the collection was created according to the orders received, whether from paying clients or harried newspaper editors. Therefore, this collection by itself will never support a complete narrative visual history of Greensboro during this roughly 50-year span.

Martin and Miller, of course, never had systematic documentation as their objective, which makes the breadth of the collection even more remarkable. Day-in and day-out, for half a century, they photographed adults and children, weddings and parties, celebrations and anniversaries, new buildings, business openings, industrial machinery, street scenes, and school life. And if they were not able to capture everything, these incredibly busy men got enough and then some. Even more, these images reflect, quite literally, the talent and artistry that propelled them to work each day. I am not certain how comfortable most of us would be if future generations could see every period, every dash, every comma, every production we had made during our business or working lives. Yet through their negatives, card files, and daily appointment books, we can reconstruct almost every minute of every day of Carol W. Martin and Malcolm A. Miller's working lives. We would all be very blessed indeed if we could look back on our own careers and life and say that we had worked as hard, produced as much, and created a legacy that will live on long after we are gone.

Current as well as future Greensboro residents owe a great debt of gratitude to these men, not only for capturing so much of our city's heritage on film, but also for carefully preserving the collection and finding it a permanent home. These images represent a tremendous body of work, a bountiful crop that the museum is committed to preserving and harvesting well into the next millennium.

This interesting night image was taken through a car windshield on West Market Street, in front of Greensboro College. Martin was documenting the reflective ability of the painted lines for a business client.

Miller and Martin stand outside of their Studio at 122 North Davie Street in 1984.

One

MARTIN AND MILLER

When Carol W. Martin and Malcolm A. Miller began their partnership full-time in February 1947, they announced that Martin's Studio was in the business of "Story Telling Photography." Young, energetic, and eager to grab all the business they could get, Martin and Miller decided to expand beyond traditional studio and portrait work. They would do it all, they said—commercial, news, industrial, advertising, candids, even social functions—and were happy to come to you. Just "Dial 7237" read their telephone book advertisement or stop by their studio at 112 East Friendly.

Carol W. Martin was already an experienced photographer when the studio opened in 1947. He was born in Roanoke, Virginia, in 1911 to James A. and Burlie Moore Martin. His father was an active, energetic man who loved the outdoors and surrounding mountains. He also was an avid hunter and often traveled long distances to find the most challenging fishing spots. This energy, enthusiasm, and love of the outdoors was a trait inherited by his youngest son, Carol. His father's greatest gift, however, might have been the folding box camera that he allowed young Carol to experiment with.

After graduating with a B.S. in Business Administration from Roanoke College in 1933, Martin worked numerous jobs before landing one he really wanted, as a reporter for the *Roanoke Times*. He started in July 1934 for $12 per week and immediately jumped into writing news articles, then added sports reporting. Since there was no staff photographer he sometimes

"Take the first call Tex!" Martin is saying to Miller on their first day of business in 1946.

took action photographs, using a 5-x-7-inch Graflex camera and verichrome film. Working nine-hour days, and every fourth week pulling the "graveyard" shift with its 12 to 13 hour days for an entire week, Martin was a well-honed photojournalist by 1937. By then, he had discovered his passion and talent, and when a former *Greensboro Daily News* reporter working at the *Times* told Martin that the *Daily News* was looking to hire their first full-time staff photographer, he jumped at the opportunity. With the $35-a-week job in hand, Martin arrived in Greensboro in the middle of January 1938. He later stated that he came here "hoping to move on to Richmond or Atlanta" and that he never thought he would want to stay in such a small town, "but I got to love this town, got married and started raising children." In fact, he met Ruth Hines, his future wife, soon after settling in at the Wesley Long apartments on North Elm Street, where she lived in an apartment building next to him.

Martin went to work fast, setting up his darkroom on the third floor of the Greensboro News Company building at Davie and Gaston (now the Cultural Arts Center at Davie and Friendly). He purchased his camera and equipment from The Art Shop—a 5-x-7-inch Kodak auto focus enlarger and a 4-x-5-inch Speed Graphic camera with a 6-inch Zeiss Tessar F 3.5 lens—designed the lab, and then hit the streets that he would come to know almost blindfolded in the next 45 years.

Always resourceful, Martin was also innovative. A year or so after his arrival, he convinced the editors of *The Greensboro Record* to publish a late Saturday sports edition. This gave Martin time to shoot football action at Carolina or Duke and send the negatives back to Greensboro where they were printed and published in the late edition. He first used a motorcycle rider and later carrier pigeons, constructing a rooftop coop to hold them. His sports photography was only one of the assignments that kept him busy, for he had to cover everything from breaking news events to "society" life. During the war, Martin edited the sports page, made photographs for both the *Daily News* and the *Record*, and worked 12 hours or more a day, six days a week. It was a busy, stressful, yet exhilarating time. Wartime rationing often required him to travel to football

This photograph, taken at the Roanoke County school races in 1937, is one of the earliest existing photojournalistic images by Carol W. Martin.

games with only four sheets of film; this earned him the nickname "one-shot," because that was about how much of a chance he had to capture the key action.

The newspaper managers allowed him to supplement his income by selling extra prints from his newspaper assignments. Many other images stuck in his mind, and years later, he compiled a long list of his memorable early news photographs, including the following: the first Greater Greensboro Open (GGO) tournament in April 1938; the 1942 Rose Bowl game held at Durham; the Biggs murder case; numerous World War II images; and prominent individuals like policeman "Sunshine" Wyrick at Jefferson Square.

Martin worked by himself until 1944, when free-lance photographer Malcolm Miller was hired to help him. Like Martin, Miller was not a native North Carolinian. He was born into a textile working family in Greenville, South Carolina, in 1917. Seeking better jobs, his mother and father moved their family of four children to the Glencoe Cotton Mills in Alamance County, near Burlington. Both worked for Glencoe until 1922, when Mrs. Miller died, a tragic experience for her family. Within a decade, Miller's father found a better job in Greensboro and moved into a Revolution Mill village house, which was near the Cone Mills plant where he worked. During the 1930s, Malcolm joined his father at the mill, working part-time between his schooling and, later, more regularly as a loom fixer. His factory work was not the only contribution he made to Cone. One day he accompanied a friend to the White Oak YMCA, and, in the darkroom at the Y, the magic of photography entered Miller's blood. He became fascinated with the whole experience and soon converted an old backyard chicken house to a "light tight" room. He carried water in by hand and slowly learned the craft and art of taking and developing photographs. He soon began taking images around town, and some were published in the Cone Mills *Textorian* newsletter.

Miller's life changed forever in July 1944, when Clarence Tucker called to say that First Lady Eleanor Roosevelt was on a layover, changing trains in Greensboro. This was an unannounced

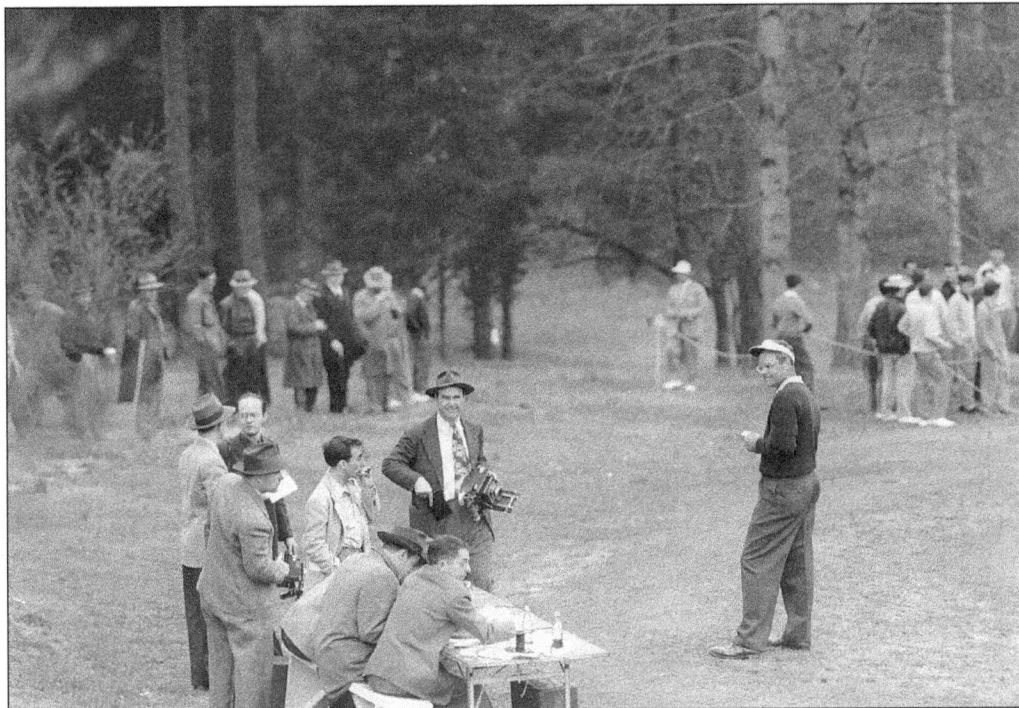

Malcolm Miller gets set for another image at an early GGO golf tournament, *c.* 1947. The golfer at right is amateur Skip Alexander. The balding man at back is sports writer and photographer John Havlicek, and sports editor Smith Barrier is talking with him.

visit, and the local newspaper editors, and thus Carol Martin, were unaware that she was in town. Miller grabbed his equipment and headed to the depot, where he found the First Lady at the Red Cross canteen, and she most graciously agreed to let him photograph her. Malcolm contacted the newspaper afterward, and his impressive images were published—for a credit line, not money—in both the morning and evening editions. A couple of weeks later, however, he cashed in when the newspaper asked him to come to work part-time to assist the overworked Martin. Thereafter, whenever someone asked him how he got his start in photography, Miller would always quip, "I tell 'em Eleanor Roosevelt got me my first job."

In fact, Miller's arrival created some early tension between the two since Martin, although swamped with work, had been earning some sizable overtime pay. But their competitiveness was mixed with good-natured banter. One day a box of textured photographic paper came into the lab and so enthralled Miller that Martin started calling him "Tex," which is the name that has stuck with him since. Thus, a friendship was born, and they soon began talking about something more.

If by 1945 Martin had not yet arrived as a photographer, he was certainly knocking on the door, both locally and statewide. He had helped to inaugurate the Carolinas Press Photographers Association in 1938 and from 1940 to 1941 served as its president. Although his contacts in the Greensboro community had come slowly, they were growing steadily. He later stated that "the older families in Greensboro were very conservative and something about news photographers they didn't like." But society page editor Anne White helped him make contacts and break the ice with them. Also, joining organizations like the Jaycees and the Greensboro Rotary Club helped to cement relationships. In fact, these growing connections helped turn Martin's thoughts to the possibility of opening his own studio.

By early 1946, Martin and Miller began discussing that very idea. Their "business plan" was simple. They figured that Martin's reputation assured steady portrait and wedding work, and

The first home of Martin's studio was behind F.W. Woolworth at 116 West Sycamore (February One Place).

industrial and business photography offered lucrative possibilities. Only William A. Roberts Film Co. was advertising locally for commercial work in 1946, and they thought that Miller could develop this end of the business.

Their dreams resulted in The Darkroom, which opened in 1946 on the second floor of a house at 116 West Sycamore (now February One Place) behind F.W. Woolworth. Martin was the majority owner, with Miller eventually owning 25% of the business. During that first year, at Miller's suggestion, they changed the business name to Martin's Darkroom, to better capitalize on Martin's name. Miller left the newspaper sometime in 1946 to help nurture the business along. They felt their way slowly, even selling camera equipment, supplies, and photo finishing for a while. Each soon realized, however, that chemicals not retailing was in their blood, so between Christmas 1946 and New Years Day, they sold all their merchandise.

Martin had planned to leave the newspaper the prior September but was persuaded to stay through the end of the football season. By then, the Darkroom's initial successes gave both Martin and Miller confidence to take the final plunge. In early 1947, they changed the business name, for the third and final time, to "Martin's Studio" and began a business career and partnership destined to change Greensboro's photographic landscape.

They were hard workers, putting in long, grueling hours, never turning away business. Much of the first year found them, on Friday and Saturday nights, taking nightclub photographs at the old Casa Blanca and Plantation Supper Club on High Point Road. This grinding work was hard on the body and also not easy on family life. Martin would later state that he had "pretty much lived my life for my family and my business," and the same could be said for Miller. They were driven to succeed, but start-up businesses usually demand all of one's time and more. Before leaving the newspaper, Martin helped break in the new photographer, Jack Moebes, who may have been even more overworked than Martin had been before Miller arrived. So the newspaper worked out a contract with Martin and Miller to continue taking the social and wedding images. Besides the money, there was the added benefit of having their credit line in the paper. This generated even more favorable publicity for the studio.

Clarence Tucker, Malcolm "Tex" Miller, and Carol Martin sit in the Gaston Street (Friendly Avenue) studio in the 1950s.

They were busy from the start and brought in Miller's brother-in-law, Clarence Tucker, who served as a lab technician until his death in 1987. As planned, Martin took most of the studio, social, and wedding images, and before long, Miller had numerous commercial accounts, including Western Electric, Jefferson Standard, Cone Mills, and Carolina Steel. There was still plenty of sharing, as each would fill in for the other, and even Tucker would occasionally move from the printing lab to the camera. Aerial photographic assignments, however, were always given to Miller, since airplane rides never appealed to Martin. They would also team up frequently on bigger shoots, like large weddings and events or anytime the heavy, bulky, 8-x-10-inch negative camera equipment was used. And for many years, Labor Day always found them in Chapel Hill shooting individual photographs for the Carolina football team.

By 1948, the studio needed bigger quarters and moved to a building at 112 East Gaston (Friendly) that had a large first-floor area that they divided into three rooms. In 1956, two more air-conditioned rooms were added in the rear, and Martin's became the first studio in Greensboro with their own color lab. They processed 4-x-5-inch Ektacolor, using a color "bucket" and a 50-gallon tank with a water chiller, and printed up to 16-x 20-inch prints. Most of the negatives they shot were 4-x-5 inch, and away from the studio they used flash bulbs, sometimes in great quantities. Large weddings usually generated a huge pile of spent bulbs, and in lieu of cleaning up themselves, they would leave a $1 bill at the bottom of the pile. From the beginning, they tried to stay on top of the latest technology and around 1948 achieved another local first when they shot a wedding using the bulb's eventual replacement, an electronic flash. Their final move came in 1966, when the new parking deck at Friendly and Davie went up, and their building had to be torn down. Luckily, they were able to find a space less than a block away at 122 North Davie, where they were to remain until they went out of business in 1992.

Throughout their business lives, both Martin and Miller pursued their own photographic interests, which helped to keep photography fresh and exciting for both of them. Miller's commercial and business contacts led to many freelance jobs, and he would often get calls from

Malcolm Miller took this image of The Three Stooges, Shemp, Moe, and Larry, at the Polio Hospital with an unknown patient around 1949.

Jefferson Standard's Joseph Bryan to do special shoots for him, including once spending an entire day with movie cowboy Gene Autry. Over the years, both Martin and Miller won photographic contests. In 1952, for example, they entered the annual Lost Colony press photographers contest and placed first and third, with Miller's image of Uppowac, the Native American medicine man, being chosen for the cover of the 1953 souvenir program.

Martin continued to be involved in state and local organizations, serving as president of the Professional Photographers of North Carolina from 1969 to 1970, which he had first joined in 1947. He and Miller became involved in the Professional Photographic Society of Greensboro and its efforts to strengthen contacts among local photographers. By the 1970s, Martin's eye was caught by the rural landscape surrounding Greensboro, which was fast disappearing. He began to spend most of his weekends riding the back roads, his favorite place being along N.C. 150 in Caswell County. Shooting in color, he processed the prints himself and began displaying these landscapes and views of barns and people in the studio's storefront window. A regional McDonald's franchise owner and his decorator saw them there in the late 1970s and started purchasing prints to decorate their restaurants throughout the state. This led to numerous sales to businesses, organizations, and individuals and helped to keep Martin's creative energies flowing well into the eighth decade of his life.

A heart attack in 1977 slowed Martin down, but Miller and Tucker took up the slack, and when Martin took his final portrait in June 1992, the business was approaching its 50,000th job. Martin told a local reporter a few weeks later that he never thought he would see the day when "we're closed" came from his lips. From his very first paid photograph in 1934 of the new rose growers club president in Roanoke until his last image on June 17th of a Jefferson-Pilot Insurance Company employee, it had been a long, determined, and creative run.

Although Martin found the technical changes in photography amazing, with its ever smaller cameras and equipment (not including digital, which would have really amazed and intrigued him), this seasoned professional's observation on the essence of the job will never age.

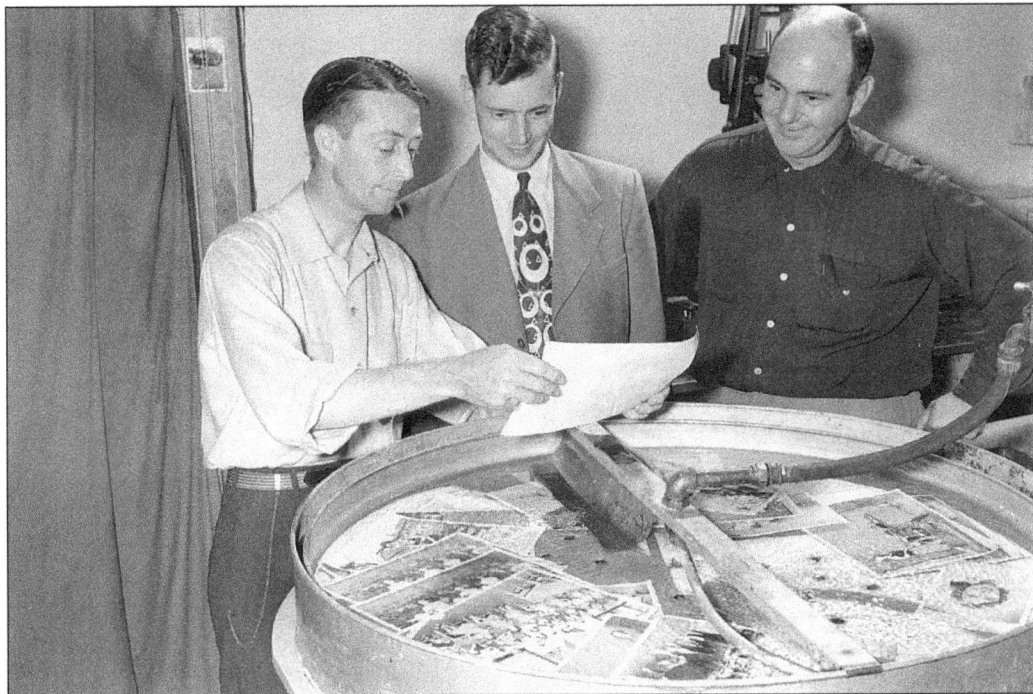

Martin and Miller examine a newly washed print with a Jefferson Standard employee in their Gaston Street lab on June 4, 1952.

"Photographers still have to use their imagination and come up with a print that will make people stop and look," he told the reporter.

Martin readily admitted to a reporter that he had always wanted to be considered the best photographer in North Carolina, but he felt the noted photojournalist Hugh Morton of Grandfather Mountain had achieved that distinction. More recently, Morton gave his own appraisal. Reflecting on their many years of friendship, Morton noted that their relationship began in 1939 when he was 18 years old and a student photographer for *The Daily Tar Heel* at the University of North Carolina (UNC). He was learning sports photography then and got to know Martin as he and all the sideline photographers jockeyed for position. "Carol became my idol as a photographer right away" states Morton. "Just watching him work the sidelines was an education" he added, " because he was just so good at what he was doing." Morton turned the table on Martin with his closing observation, that, in his opinion, North Carolina has never seen a finer photographer than Carol W. Martin.

Above all else, what comes through clearly when looking back at the work and careers of Martin and Miller is the great love and dedication that each had for the art and craft of photography. To grind away day after day for over 45 years, consistently producing high-quality work, requires both dedication and love. It may also take a continuing desire to improve, to experience once more the thrill of the next snap of the shutter, to never lose the wondrous feeling of anticipation as another latent image emerges from its chemical bath. This magic never seems to have left either of them. In fact, when asked what was his all-time best photograph Martin never hesitated to reply, "maybe the next one."

Carol Martin takes a quick break at the Debutante Ball in Raleigh in September 1946.

Two

PHOTOJOURNALISM

Good newspaper photographs grab your attention saying "read this story first," which is exactly what Carol Martin's 1944 "Fire on Gorrell Street" image on page 22 does. You can almost feel the heat and smell the smoke drifting out of the image, and you want to know what happened. Newspapers, however, have not always contained photographs. In fact, it was not until the late 1880s, when the halftone screening process was perfected, that photographs began to appear more regularly. Greensboro newspapers contained few if any photographs until well after that date. Although more and more graphics were being used, they were usually drawings of people or business advertisements. When photographs started to appear locally after 1900, they still tended to be static portraits of people or business locations. The *Greensboro Telegram*, established in 1897, and *The Greensboro Daily News*, formed in 1909, were the local leaders in what we would today call photojournalism. One of the first dramatic images published locally was a 1911 picture of the famous Triangle Shirtwaist Co. fire on March 25th in New York City, which the *Daily News* ran on March 29th on page one. The *Telegram* changed formats a few weeks later and began subscribing to a telegraphic wire service, resulting in a dramatic increase in their use of photographs. Local residents very quickly began seeing the famous and infamous, along with big doses of sports photography.

It took many more years, both nationally and locally, for photojournalism to become what we would recognize today. By the time Martin came to the *Daily News* in 1938 (his earliest credit line appears on January 20th under an Elon College basketball image), photography was a major drawing card for readers. During Martin's era, if photography had yet to displace words, it was well on its way to becoming a dominant communication tool.

Douglas "Wrong Way" Corrigan received a hero's welcome in Greensboro on August 27, 1938. Only six weeks before, unable to get official flight approval in his attempt to duplicate Lindbergh's Atlantic crossing of 1927, Corrigan left New York and "mistakenly" flew all the way to Ireland. He told officials when he landed that he meant to fly to Los Angeles but had misread his compass. The country loved it and was hardly surprised when he admitted years later that it had all been an intentional "mistake."

Postmaster General James A. Farley came to Newton, North Carolina, on April 26, 1938, to open a new post office. Although by this date North Carolina had seen the worst of the economic dislocations brought on by the Great Depression, all federal public works projects were highly coveted and appreciated during these lean years.

The *Greensboro Daily News* published this image on October 7, 1938, with the following caption: "Crowd is seen here in front of High Point city hall awaiting return of James Godwin, who escaped from Davidson county jail last Monday and is charged with subsequently murdering Donald Moss of High Point, who was shot while sitting in his car on Pine street Monday night." James F. Godwin was convicted and executed in Raleigh on September 22, 1939, becoming (as of 1999) one of the 370 men (282 black, 83 white, 5 Native American) and 3 women (2 black, 1 white) to be executed in North Carolina since 1910.

This locomotive ran through an open switch at the Southern Railway Depot on July 30, 1941. The coal tender was damaged, as was the first open car, but the other 58 cars were unscratched, and no one on the train was seriously injured.

Sheriff John Story (left) and his deputies busted up this Guilford County still around 1939. "Bootlegging" has a long history in North Carolina, and even though Prohibition was popular in the State (Will Rogers once told a Raleigh audience that North Carolinians would continue to vote "dry" as long as they can "stagger to the polls."), it only intensified during the 1920s and 1930s. Yet even with the repeal of the 18th Amendment in 1933 and the creation of the Alcohol and Beverage Commission board in 1937, moonshiners refused to go away, and the state still spends between $300,000 and $500,000 per year chasing after them.

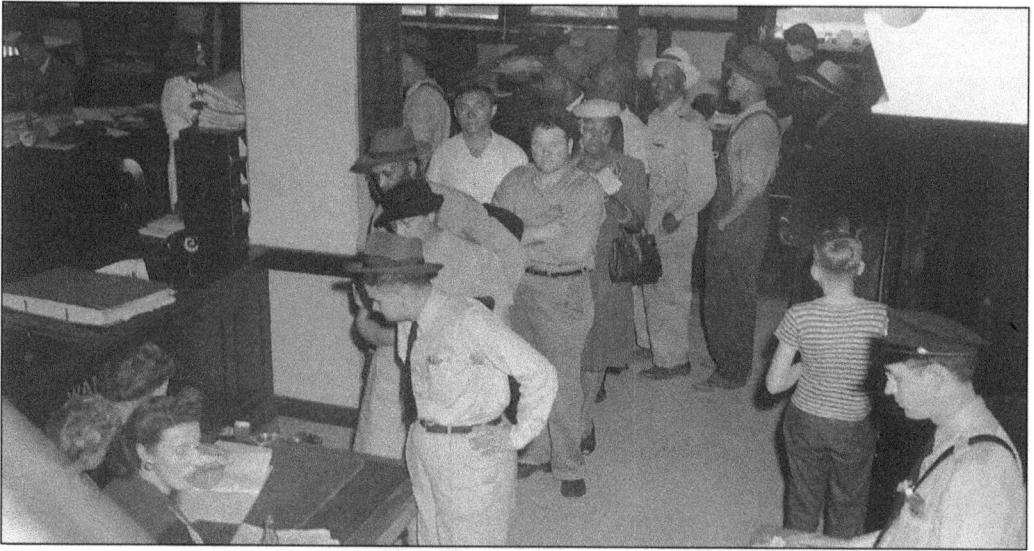

Citizens could vote at the courthouse during the 1940s. It was not that old of a custom for women, however, who had only been voting since passage of the 19th Amendment in 1920. African-Americans, on the other hand, although legally able to vote since the 15th Amendment of 1870, had not always been able to freely exercise this right in the South. In Greensboro and Guilford County, according to the noted black political leader and educator Vance Chavis, whites had not, at least not overtly, tried to discourage blacks from voting. In fact, African-American candidate Robert C. Sharp received 31% of the popular city-wide vote in the 1943 council race, coming in 9th out of 12 candidates. And in 1951, Dr. William Hampton was elected to the council with 51% of the popular vote.

Fort Bragg was the largest artillery post in the world during WWII, covering 122,000 acres, with 3,135 buildings. Carol Martin captured these soldiers in action during Army Day on April 6, 1942. Fort Bragg, which was one of 21 military installations in North Carolina, zoomed from a 1940 capacity of 5,400 men to over 100,000 by war's end.

When Martin took this image, soldiers had just begun arriving at Basic Training Center #10 (BTC#10). It opened on March 1, 1943, at the corner of Bessemer and Summit Avenues and trained over 87,000 Army Air Force soldiers by May 1944. The 650-acre base then became an Overseas Replacement Depot (ORD), processing an additional 250,000 soldiers—most headed to the air war in Europe—before the base closed in late 1946. BTC#10-ORD was the only base operating within the city limits of an American town.

By 1942, wartime food stamps were a requirement in Greensboro stores. During WWII, shortages, both real and anticipated, as well as the desire to combat inflation brought about the rationing of goods and control of prices under the Office of Price Administration (OPA). The correct numbers of stamps or coins were needed to buy foods such as vegetables, butter, coffee, canned goods, and meat. Although shortages were not as bad in America as elsewhere, civilians were relieved in late 1945 when 43 months of rationing ended for most products.

On January 14, 1944, four houses were destroyed in the 1000 block of Gorrell Street when a gasoline tanker truck's axle broke, causing the trailer to drag and produce sparks that set off an

explosion. The flames spread 300 feet, burning through fire hose lines with heat so intense it could be felt two blocks away. Luckily, no one was seriously injured.

Malcolm Miller took this image of First Lady Eleanor Roosevelt at the Southern Railroad Depot in Greensboro on July 24, 1944. (She autographed it on a later visit.). He had received a tip from Clarence Tucker that Mrs. Roosevelt had stopped unexpectedly in Greensboro. Because Carol Martin was not there, Miller offered this image to the *Greensboro Daily News*, and they published it the next day. This led, a few weeks later, to a job offer and to Miller's lifetime quip when asked how he got his start in photography. "I tell 'em Eleanor Roosevelt got me my first job."

Shown here in February 1944 are Sheriff John Story and a deputy guarding William Dalton Biggs, his brother Elmer Hardie Biggs, and John Edgar Messer. All three were given the death sentence for the 1943 pistol slaying of E.J. Swanson, and they were executed in Raleigh on March 9, 1945.

24

June 23, 1944, was a lucky day for Nancy Souther, and it shows. She was one of the fortunate ones to buy these illegally made wartime nylon stockings, which were being sold at the post office after having been confiscated by U.S. Marshal Edney Ridge.

An officer salutes as President Roosevelt's funeral train passes through Greensboro shortly before 1 a.m. on April 14, 1945. Thousands of citizens stood along the tracks, including honor guards from ORD, Fort Bragg, and Camp Butner. Two green and gold Southern Railway engines pulled the train, its last car fully illuminated with the raised bronze casket flanked at each corner by a serviceman in full dress uniform. When asked about this historic moment in 1995, Carol Martin told a reporter, "Not a word was spoken as the train rolled by . . . the atmosphere was very heavy."

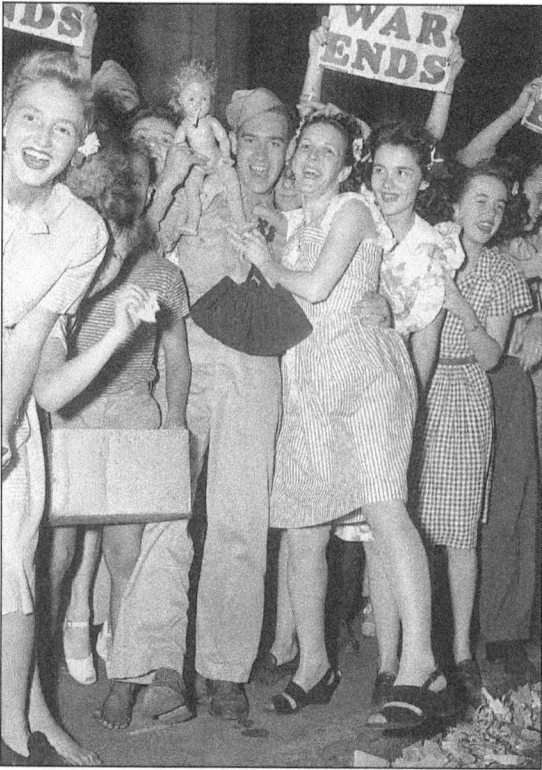

The night of August 14, 1945, was an historic moment in Greensboro's and the country's history. Noted the *Greensboro Daily News*, "Four days of pent up tension burst forth in wild shouts, blaring horns and jangling cowbells as half the population of Greensboro congregated on Elm Street within two minutes after President Truman's announcement last night that the Japanese have accepted allied surrender terms." Housewife Beth Puckett caught the raw power of this moment when she wrote the next day to her husband Lewis, "It's over . . . I just keep repeating 'it's over'. I've been trying to analyze the emotions but I can't yet. Relief, joy, thanksgiving—all mixed up beyond belief."

These 1946 workers at Mock-Judson-Voeheringer are hanging Arthur T. Sakowski, their personnel manager, in effigy. Attempts to organize Southern textile workers by the Congress of Industrial Organizations (CIO) and the Textile Workers Union of America—especially in 1946 with their massive "Operation Dixie" campaign—picked up speed after the war, with labor strife and sometimes violence erupting between management and workers. The 1946 effort was a notable failure, but, in general, union organizing efforts have never proved very successful in the South.

Severe flooding, not drought, prompted this photograph of Lake Brandt on September 25, 1947. A coastal storm dumped nearly 8 inches of rain in 24 hours, causing the dam to break. Ironically, all this water forced Greensboro into an emergency water rationing situation, since Lake Brandt was the city's only reservoir. Quick action brought repairs to the dam by late in the day on September 26th.

The March of Dimes fundraising walk, sponsored by the Junior Chamber of Commerce, was headed to High Point when it passed down West Market Street on January 22, 1949. President Roosevelt established the March of Dimes in 1939 to help raise research funds to find a cure for polio. After the Salk vaccine achieved that goal, the March of Dimes changed its mission in 1958 to raising funds and awareness about birth defects. This is still its focus today.

When Western Electric purchased the Pomona Manufacturing Company buildings at Spring Garden and Merritt Drive in 1951, it brought with it not only good jobs but also a union work force. When the Communications Workers of America (CWA) went on strike for "better working conditions" in April 1952, Greensboro witnessed an unusual sight. Three years later, the CWA undertook a more successful strike of 72 days after Southern Bell's failed attempt to enforce a new contract banning all strikes.

Junius Irving Scales is seen entering the courtroom in Greensboro on April 12, 1955. In *Scales vs. United States*, Scales—the son of the noted local real estate developer A.M. Scales—was convicted for violating the Smith Act, which made it a crime to belong to organizations that advocated the violent overthrow of the government. Scales, who had joined the Communist Party while at UNC during the 1940s, had his conviction overturned but was retried and convicted again in 1958. He did not begin serving his six-year term until October 1961, after the U.S. Supreme Court ruled that the Smith Act was constitutional.

Three

AROUND TOWN

Who remembers Friendly Shopping Center before the Center, 5¢ hamburgers at Jim's Lunch on "Hamburger Square," or Elm Street packed day and night with automobiles, people, and businesses? If you have forgotten or perhaps never saw these things, Martin and Miller were there to capture these memories and more. It is unlikely, however, that Martin took any of the aerial photographs, for as partner Malcolm Miller remembers, "Carol never had the stomach for high flying photography so he would always make sure that I got those assignments." Yet whether above town or at street level, these images provide a clear view into a 20th-century landscape that continued to change even as Martin and Miller worked.

This image of "Hamburger Square" was taken around 1941. The 5¢ hamburgers at Jim's Lunch and the California Sandwich Shop generated the name that is still in use today, long after those inexpensive eateries disappeared. The traffic circle, or "roundabout," in the foreground was one of several created during these years.

The Greensboro Coliseum, designed by the local architectural firm McMinn, Norfleet & Wicker, is seen here under construction on March 5, 1959. It was dedicated on October 24, 1959, and the first sporting event was a Greensboro Generals hockey game on November 11. Over 4,600 fans came to see the Generals defeat the Washington Presidents 4 to 1, breaking a six-game losing streak. Alan Baty has the honor of having scored the first goal in Greensboro history. Go Generals!

Although a primary four-lane traffic artery in 1961, High Point Road still retained its suburban character when Miller took this image on October 19, 1961. With the arrival of the Greensboro Coliseum in 1959, however, the area became the hub of sports and entertainment activity. The resulting stores, restaurants, and fast-food eateries soon displaced the trees and vacant land.

In the 1940s, the business community and neighborhoods on East Market Street, which urban renewal projects in the 1960s displaced, were still visible beyond the railroad tracks. The Gate City Motor Company building and Duke Power's huge gas storage tanks (the large one held 200,000 cubic feet of gas) are visible on the left. East Gaston (now Friendly Avenue) dead-ended there and would not be extended eastward until the 1960s.

The coming of the new U.S. Post Office on East Market, seen here under construction in April 1965, meant hundreds of high-paying jobs. However, the wider roads and new buildings also destroyed the small shops and stores that had formed the core of a thriving African-American community.

31

You could only cruise Elm Street by heading north after the street became one-way in 1949. By the 1970s, this crowded, lively scene—seen here on January 11, 1958—had become a historical curiosity, as most cars were then heading to the suburban shopping centers: Summit (open in 1950), Friendly (open in 1957), Golden Gate (open in 1961), and Four Seasons Mall (open in 1974).

This rare view (at top), taken April 6, 1951, shows the future site of Friendly Shopping Center. Edward Benjamin's tree-lined drive (far right) can be seen here and can still be walked today in front of the Harris Teeter store. Although houses in the Starmount area across the road began to be built in the 1930s, most were constructed after WWII, when the earlier plans of Edward and Blanche Sternberger Benjamin reached their full fruition. Friendly Shopping Center opened, with 25,000 shoppers, on August 1, 1957, two weeks before Miller went up to make this image (below, from opposite direction) on August 16th.

This view of Interstate 40 at Highway 68 was taken on September 16, 1963. When the interstate opened in the 1960s, this area was still surrounded by a rural landscape.

Taken at 4 p.m. on March 19, 1956, this view of "rush hour" traffic on what appears to be Highway 29 North certainly suggests that, in some respects at least, the idea of the "good old days" is not totally myth.

"Trust your car to the man who wears the star" would later become a popular advertisement for Texaco. People pulling into this station at the corner of West Lee and Tate on May 15, 1952, put their trust in the hands of Walter C. Upchurch and Oliver P. Barney. There had been a gas

station at this site since the early 1920s, and one remained there until around 1963, although Upchurch and Barney moved to Lee and Aycock in 1955.

The Glenwood Park Sanitarium—"dedicated to the care and treatment of mild mental, nervous, and habit cases . . . rest from worry, overwork, or care"—opened in 1918, having succeeded the Telfair Sanitarium founded in 1903. In 1978, Glenwood became the Crawford Treatment Center, operating until the mid-1990s.

In December 1950, Christmas shoppers could buy nylon hose for $1 at the Fashion Shop, a 63-piece set of Noritake china for $55 at Belks, and a good silk tie for dad for $1.39 at Meyer's Department Store. This region was already a major retail market, home to approximately 1,500 retail and service businesses, with sales totaling close to $873 million within a 50-mile radius of Greensboro.

Martin's caught this snow scene at the Keeley Institute on February 27, 1952. A sanitarium, or hospital for alcoholics and drug addicts, Keeley was located at present-day Blandwood from 1897 until it closed in 1961. Under the early directorship of William H. Osborn, and later his wife and brother-in-law, Keeley treated patients from across the United States and around the world. Osborn became the first commissioner of the Internal Revenue Service in 1913.

Smaller grocery stores, like the Cheek Mercantile Store in Pleasant Garden, were still the norm in April 1947. The range of products was great, but, as seen here, a whole "department" might consist of only a couple of shelves.

This aerial view of Greensboro (Grimsley) High School was taken around 1949, looking west. When the school moved to this site in 1929, it was billed as Greensboro's "million dollar" high school and opened with only three buildings: Old Science (at bottom), the main building, and the cafeteria behind it. The vocational building, at right, opened in 1942. At top left are the auxiliary gym (1939) and the original gymnasium, which was replaced with the new gym in 1954. The distinctive covered walkways were added during the 1930s.

High Point Road, in April 1953 (and on the opposite page, from the same spot in 1999), retained this relatively bucolic appearance until Interstate 40 opened in the early 1960s, and Joe Koury began his Four Seasons complex several years later. The building, at left behind the trees, is the then-popular Plantation Supper Club, which was managed by Fred Koury, Joe's cousin. Nationally known singers and groups performed there from about 1950 until the early 1970s. During the era of segregation, popular black performers played to all-white audiences at the Plantation and then usually took their act to A.G. Faucette's El Rocco Club on East Market to entertain African-American crowds.

Four

Now and Then

On March 5, 1999, this author gathered together a number of photographs taken by Martin and Miller decades ago and went back to the same spot to see how things had changed. It was an exhilarating experience. In some instances, the changes were monumental and in others, not so much. In every instance, it brought forth a powerful feeling of connectivity, both to the past and to these two photographers. It is impossible on a printed page to duplicate the feeling, but the reader can still appreciate the changes to our urban landscape that these photographs document.

This 1999 image of the 3600 block of High Point Road, looking east, when compared with the image at the bottom of the opposite page taken from the same location, shows how drastically this road has changed in 46 years.

In 50 years, Hamburger Square has changed a lot, with traffic circles or "roundabouts" and the Hotel Clegg (in 1961) having long since disappeared. But in 1999, you can still "pay less" at Blumenthal's like you could in the 1940s. The odd-looking metal "umbrella" in the traffic circle flashed right arrows to approaching drivers, reminding them which direction they needed to enter the circle.

Commerce Place long ago ceased to be a major shopping street, as these members of the Greensboro Motorcycle Club in 1947 would quickly realize today. Motorcycle clubs and riding became popular after the war when a lot of free spirit "letting loose" from the Depression and war years took place. Although these riders certainly did not have shopping on their minds that morning, the A&P Supermarket and Greensboro Curb Market were normally very busy during regular hours. Visible at the back left (lower image) is the domed Greensboro Pubic Library building. It served as the city's white library from 1906 until 1939, when it moved to the current historical museum building. The old library was used as West Market Street Methodist Church's annex until it was torn down for the new education building (upper image) in 1950.

The racetrack at the fairgrounds, seen here on May 23, 1946, disappeared with the coming of the Greensboro Coliseum in 1959. This image actually represents some of the earliest post-WWII action since all organized motorcycle racing was suspended during the war. The American Motorcycle Association (AMA) geared up quickly in 1946, and, thereafter, dirt-track racing grew in spectator and competitor popularity. In 1999, Grand National motorcycle racing celebrated its 45th anniversary, making it one of the oldest competitive racing series in the world.

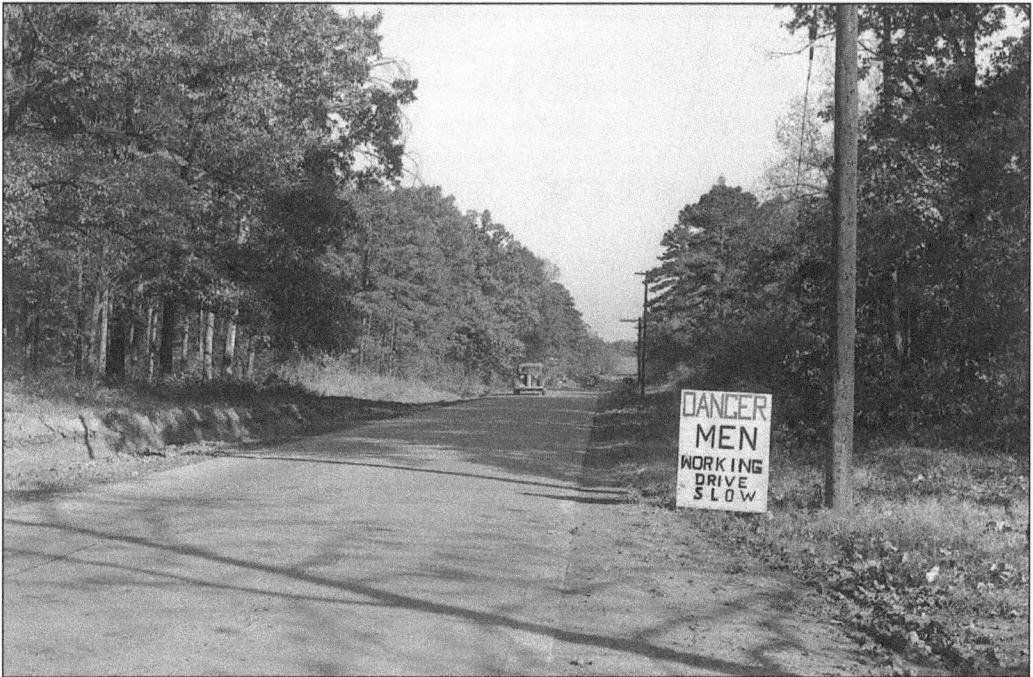

Bessemer Avenue, looking north from Summit Avenue, changed radically between 1942 and 1999. In fact, the greatest change occurred shortly after Carol Martin made this earlier image, since he had gone out to photograph the road before the Army Air Force began constructing the military base on this site. When Basic Training Center #10 opened in March 1943, a large military entrance gate was built at about this same spot, and access to Bessemer Avenue was closed to the general public until the base closed in late 1946.

The construction of a stadium at Greensboro (Grimsley) High School was approved in 1939, with excavation beginning in November 1941, just weeks before Pearl Harbor. Work Projects Administration workers moved most of the dirt, but students in physical education classes also helped. It was paid for by the Federal Works Projects Administration, the Greensboro School Board, and private bonds. WWII caused a delay in construction, and the stadium was not opened until 1949. Its 10,000 seats make it the largest on-campus high school stadium in North Carolina. When long-time coach and educator Bob Jamieson retired in 1975, the stadium was named in his honor.

The view looking west at Market and Elm has undergone major changes in the past 50 years. The Jefferson-Pilot building on the right, the West Market Street Methodist Church in the distance, and buildings in that 200 block are about the only structures still standing. The officer at attention in the intersection is Charles "Sunshine" Wyrick (see p. 85), who entertained citizens and kept traffic moving at this busy crossroads during the 1930s and 1940s.

Greensboro had 293 miles of roads when these Thompson-Arthur Construction workers began installing curbs in the 900 block of Julian Street in September 1953 (1,069 miles paved and 5.4 miles unpaved in 1999). However, 110 miles were unpaved, with most of these being in the poorer areas of east Greensboro. Small stores, like the Happy Hill Grocery at Julian and Best, were very important neighborhood anchors. By the 1990s, however, this area, known as "The Hill," had become the most notorious drug, prostitution, and crime-ridden area in the city. Improvements finally came when Project Homestead helped redeveloped this section as "Benson Heights," building new low and middle-income housing, attracting owners instead of absentee landlords, and giving the residents a vested interest in their neighborhood.

The amphitheater at Lindley Elementary School has long since been silent, except for its current use as a great sledding hill during snows. On May 8, 1946, however, the crowds were packed onto the grass steps to watch the yearly May Day exercises. Lindley, which opened in 1928, is named for John Van Lindley, a horticulturist, businessman, and civic leader. Lindley Park was also named for him after he donated the land for its development.

East Market Street was a two-lane road before urban renewal of the 1960s turned it into a multi-lane highway. One popular spot near the Agricultural & Technical College (University) campus was the Half Moon Cafeteria at 1109 E. Market. On the spot of the old Half Moon today is the Hayes-Taylor YMCA, which has continued to expand since its opening at 1101 E. Market in 1939.

The remnants of the old beach and concrete pier at Lake Hamilton are clearly visible today. The lake was a central attraction of the Hamilton Lakes community, which was first incorporated by developer A.M. Scales in the early 1920s and featured parks, a golf course, and lakes. It remained a separate corporate body until it merged with Greensboro on July 1, 1957.

The site of the present-day Olive Garden restaurant at 3000 High Point Road has hosted a number of eating establishments since the 1950s. One of the most popular was Honey's Drive-In, seen here on August 15, 1961. The tower in the rear is the "Sky Castle," which was originally erected by McClure's Restaurant during the mid-1950s. Radio announcers from WBIG began taking requests and spinning records there, but McClure's, wanting to draw a younger crowd to its drive-in operation, changed to WCOG, which was attracting a growing teenage audience with its rock-and-roll format.

L. Richardson Memorial Hospital, designed by noted architect Charles C. Hartmann, opened at 603 South Benbow Road in May 1927. It was the first modern African-American hospital in Greensboro's history. The Greensboro Negro Hospital Association raised $100,000 to build it, with half of that amount coming from the Richardson family: Mrs. Lunsford Richardson and her son H. Smith made the donation in honor of her husband, the founder of Vick Chemical Company. The hospital stayed at this location until a new building was opened in 1966. In 1993, "L. Rich" was sold to Vencor, and the old building became a nursing home. It closed in 1996, and Project Homestead is currently planning to convert it into a low-income retirement community.

Comparing Holden Road in 1948 and 1999 shows that this busy north-south traffic artery has long since lost its rural character. In 1948, most of Holden—seen below near Madison Avenue, looking south toward West Market—was outside the city limits. This section of Holden did not become a part of Greensboro until Hamilton Lakes was incorporated in 1957.

54

Five

SCHOOL LIFE

Martin and Miller photographed all kinds of school events from the elementary grades to college level, but their primary clients over the years were Greensboro (Grimsley) High School, Woman's College (University of North Carolin Greensboro), and Greensboro College. No matter where you went to school, however, this small selection of images will probably transport you back a few years in time.

Can you remember jumping rope at recess and forgetting about class for a while; the fear yet exhilaration over the freedom-to-come that driver's training promised; the reckless abandon and great fun at sock hops and school dances; the pristine white belts and bright shinny badges of the School Patrol; the cheers, the noise, the intense anticipation of victory at afternoon pep rallies; the school assemblies, the laughter, the pranks, the fright on test days, and the many, many friends you made? These photographs will probably remind you that your school years were some of the most stressful, yet some of the best of your life.

Aycock Junior High School safety patrol guards do their job in May 1950.

These students in Mrs. Johnson's class at Lindley Elementary School show off their creations on April 25, 1949.

This photograph of a Junior Red Cross workshop class at Lincoln Street School was taken on November 18, 1953. Lincoln, which opened in 1949, was the only African-American junior high school in Greensboro's segregated public school system of the 1950s.

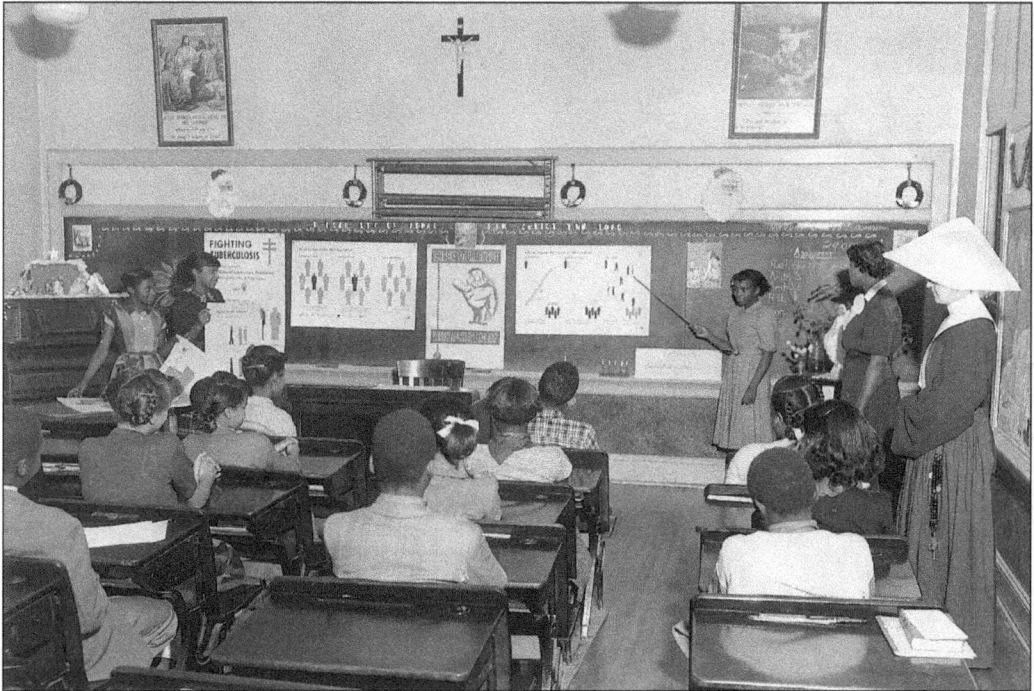

These Catholic school students are pictured on December 5, 1951. Saint Mary's Catholic Mission School opened around 1949, but for most of its history, African-American students knew the school at 1410 Gorrell Street as Our Lady of The Miraculous Medal School.

If you had asked these Aycock Junior High School students in May 1950 what they liked best about school, they probably would have screamed "Recess!" This free time was not only important for the exercise but also for the socialization skills that were learned. Of course a big benefit for the teachers was that recess burned up a lot of excess energy!

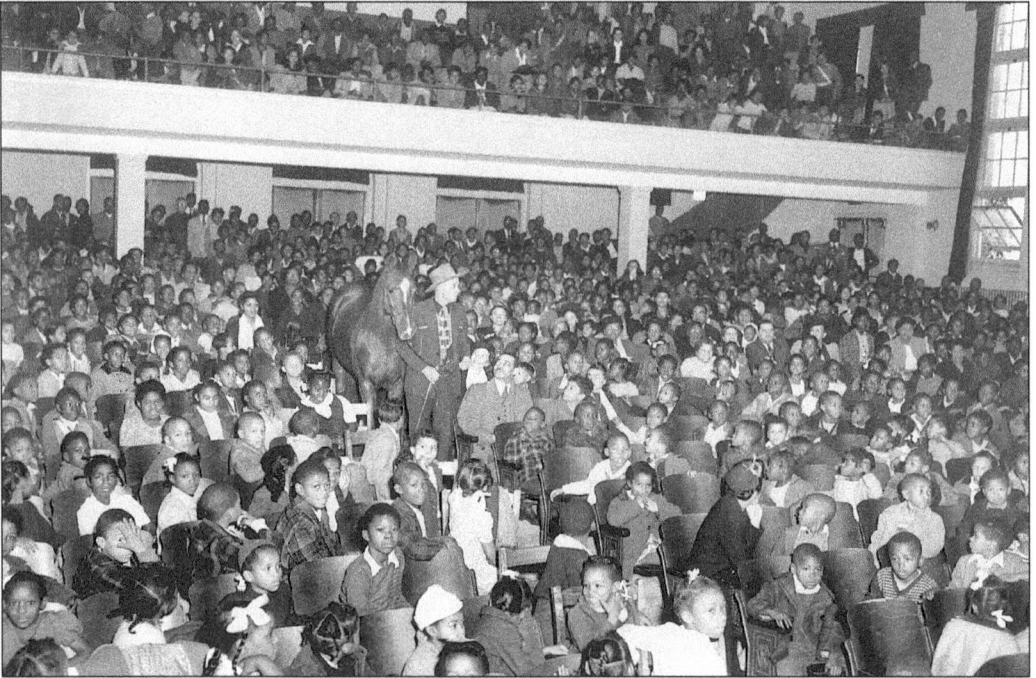

"Gallant Bess" created a lot of excitement when she visited Greensboro on December 13, 1946. Bess, the horse star of Metro-Goldwyn-Mayer's 1946 film *Gallant Bess*, came to Greensboro to promote the film. In this WWII movie, Bess was nursed back to health by a young soldier, became the unit mascot, and ended up saving the soldier's life.

When Martin's snapped this image at Jesse Wharton School on May 5, 1948, the Greensboro Public Library's bookmobile had been in operation for 22 years. It was not until the next year that the delivery of books and reading materials to the African-American community began. The countywide bookmobile lasted until the early 1990s, when it was replaced with the mobile "Cheer Service," which brings library materials to children's day care centers.

Miss Elanor Dare Taylor gets driving instructions around 1945. Driver's training has been a rite of passage for teenagers for decades, whether taught at school or privately. It became more formalized in 1957, when the North Carolina General Assembly provided license fee money to support school-based training.

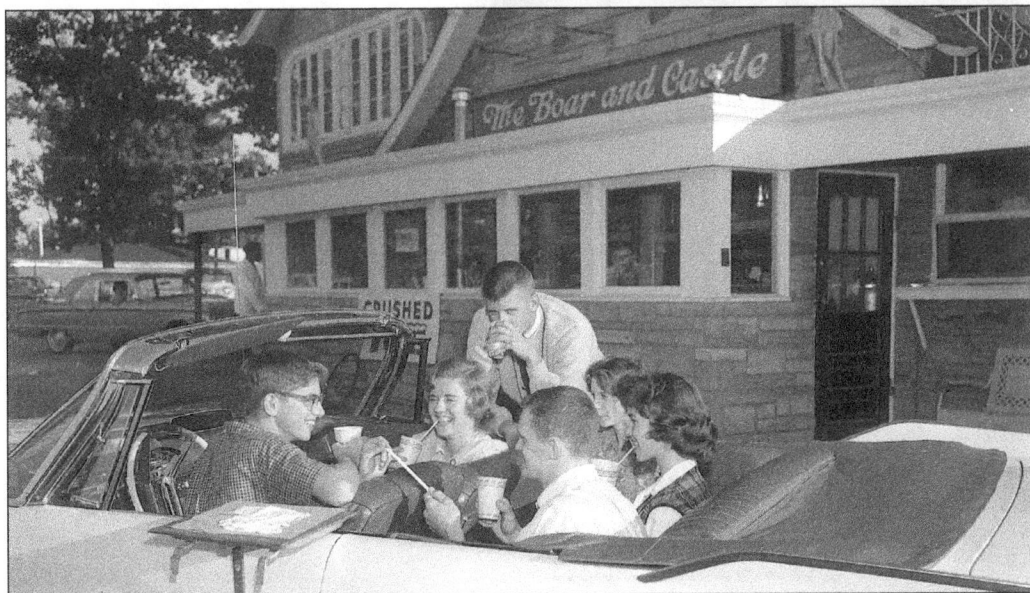

Greensboro (Grimsley) High School students relax at The Boar & Castle on October 6, 1961. The Castle opened on West Market Street in 1937 and soon became a popular eating establishment, especially for young, mobile, "cruising" teenagers and college students. Most people have long forgotten that the Castle, which closed around 1980, was the site of a golf driving range from 1938 to 1942.

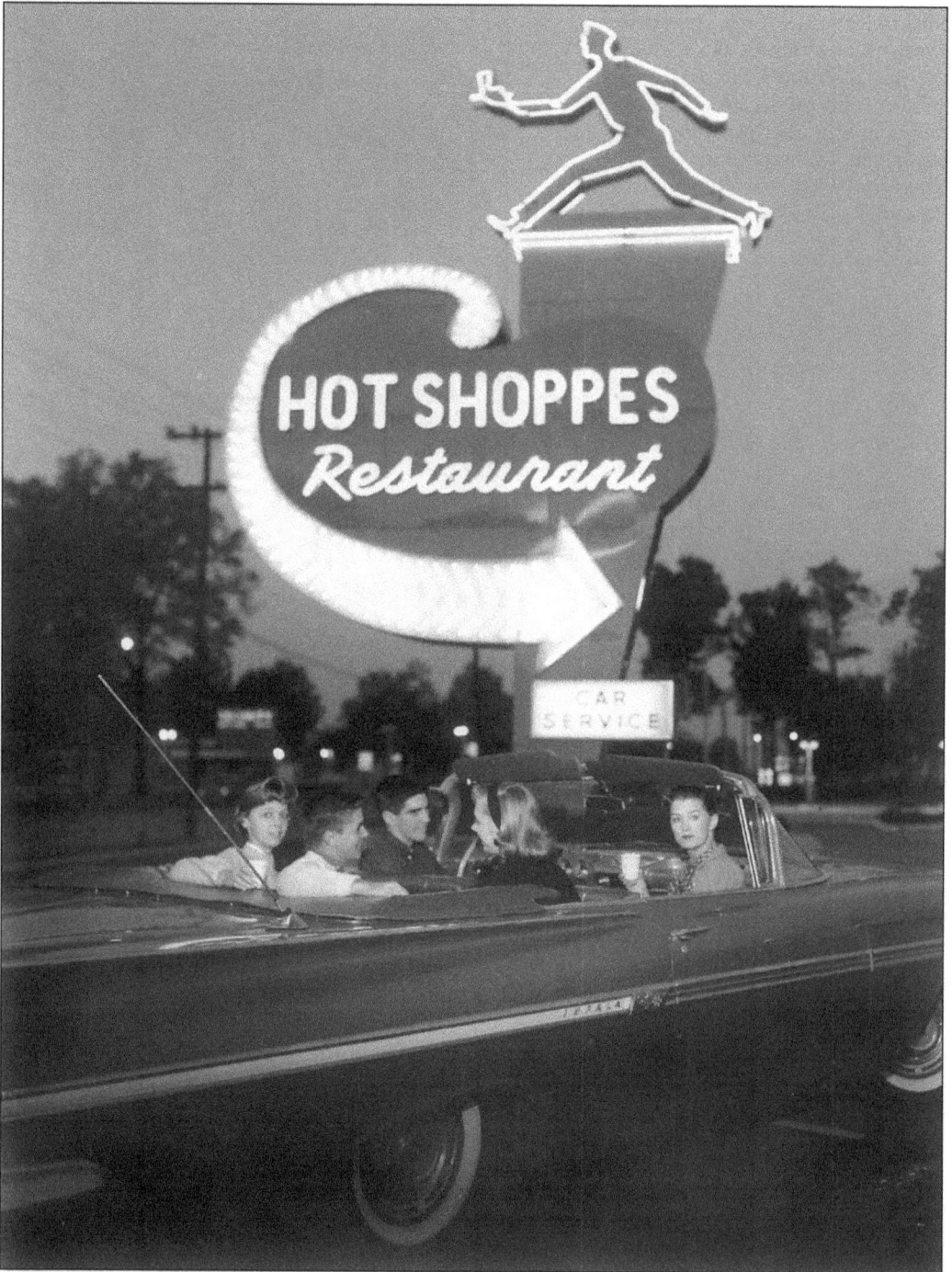

When these students pulled into the Hot Shoppes Restaurant at 1116 Summit Avenue on November 5, 1958, they may have ordered the famous "Mighty Mo" hamburger. The "Colossus of the Sandwich World" was the most popular item on their "Food for the Whole Family" menu. Hot Shoppes was a restaurant chain created by Bill Marriott in Washington, D.C., in the 1950s and was the forerunner to today's Marriott conglomerate.

The Boar and Castle was a favorite of young and old alike, as these Greensboro Senior High teachers would have attested on November 5, 1958. They are, from left to right, Robert L. "Lody" Glenn, Miss Mary Ellen Blackmon, Mrs. Jean Davis Newman, Mr. J. Stanley "Jabbo" Johnson, Miss Eula Tuttle, and Mr. Herbert Hazelman. The Castle was demolished on January 1, 1981.

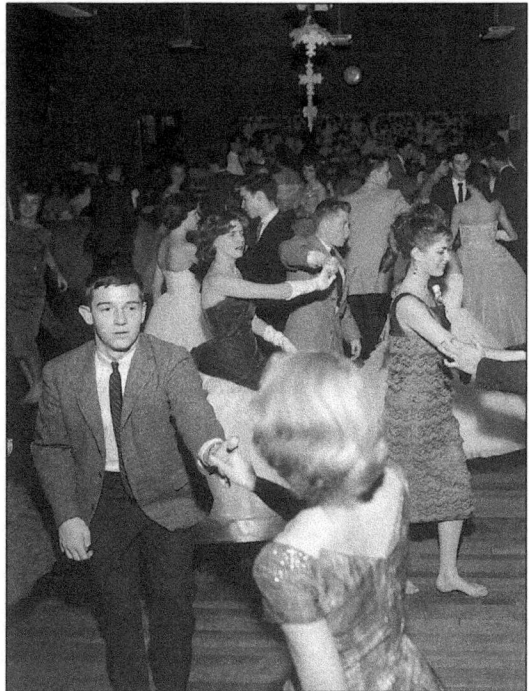

The mid-winter dance for Curry High School was held on January 10, 1959, at the Vick's Clubhouse on Milton Street. Curry was one of five high schools in Greensboro, the others being Senior (Grimsley), Page, Dudley, and Notre Dame (Catholic). Pictured here, in the foreground, is John Forbis, the future mayor of Greensboro (1981–1987), dancing with his future wife, Miss Ginny Robinson.

Greensboro has the distinction of having been the site of the first McDonald's in North Carolina, which opened at this Summit Avenue location on September 30, 1959. Six weeks later, these Greensboro High School students decided to sample its 15¢ hamburgers, 10¢ fries, and 20¢ milk shakes. McDonald's became a popular hangout, at least for white students; like all

the city's restaurants, it remained segregated until after May 1963, when local civil rights protests finally opened up all eating establishments to anyone who could pay. Pictured from left to right are Billy Bright, M. Karnes, Gene Blair, Patsey Jones, Helen Alford, and Buster Wales.

Students at Dudley High School were entertained by a marionette show on March 20, 1946. Marionettes, which are puppets moved by string or wire from above, are an art and entertainment form that date to the ancient world.

These young women are practicing their sewing skills in a Red Cross sewing class at Dudley High School on March 19, 1948. Whether they became future seamstresses or homemakers, sewing was an extremely important skill learned by most young women until more recent decades.

Page High School cheerleaders "pep" up the student body before a game in 1968. Page was opened in 1957 as Greensboro's second all-white high school. It very quickly became successful both in scholastics and athletics.

These young women from Greensboro College are finding safety in numbers as they enjoy the snow on the front lawn along West Market Street around 1942. Greensboro College was an all-female college when it was founded by the Methodist Church in 1838 and became co-educational in 1954.

These Greensboro Evening College students were sitting in front of the college at 519 W. Washington on September 5, 1952. Located at the corner of Spring Street (the present site of the Guilford Technical Community College building and across from the Weaver Center), the college was founded in 1948 by the Greensboro Chamber of Commerce to make business and technical training more easily available. The school merged with Guilford College in 1953.

These men were definitely "imported" for this March 1960 dance in the Elliot Hall ballroom at Woman's College. The school did not become co-educational until it became UNC Greensboro in 1963.

Six

CHILDREN

Being a parent does not make you a better photographer, but it does offer a different perspective. With several children between them, Martin and Miller certainly had many chances to experience the world from different angles, and their photographs of children evidence this point of view. Some of these unknown faces will simply bring a smile, such as the nine babies at the Schoolfield birthday party or young Norwood's propeller cap. And perhaps, you might remember the small gauge railroad at Country Park or maybe you once met Old Rebel and Pecos Pete?

But childhood can just as easily bring pain and fright, as graphically depicted in the disturbing images at the Polio Hospital in 1952. After one of his daughters contracted the disease, Martin agreed to photo-document the hospital and its patients for the opportunity to visit with her more frequently. Thus, it became more than just another job, which seems to have been the case with many of the children's images taken by Martin's Studio over the years.

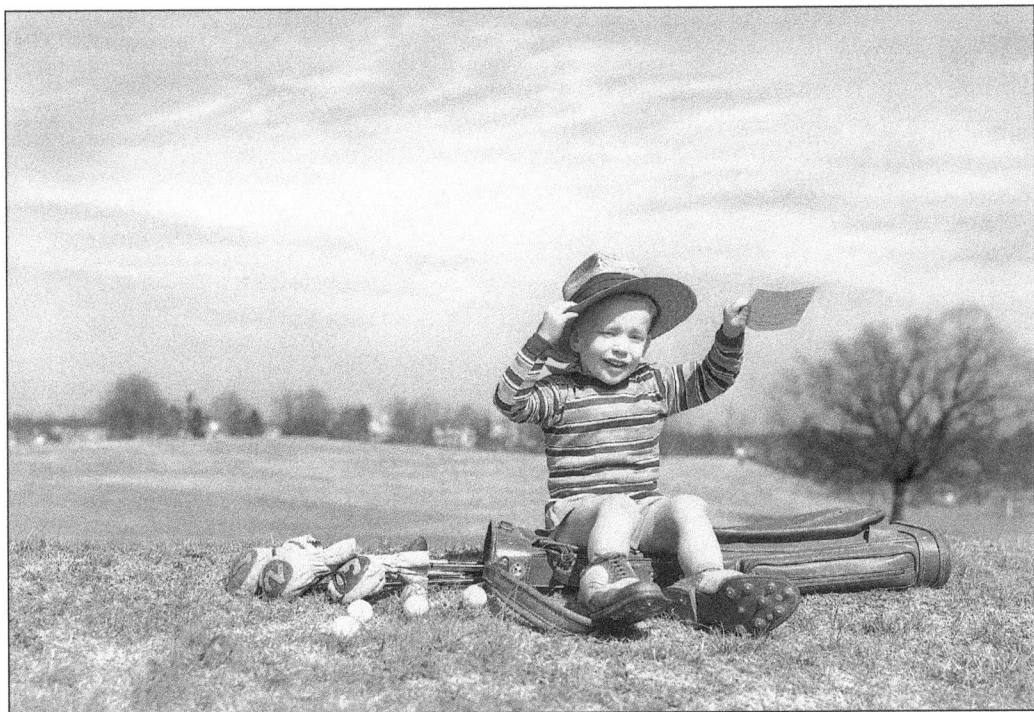

Bill Barrier, the son of the noted newspaper sports editor and columnist Smith Barrier, poses as a budding sportswriter and golfer in February 1946. His father's sports columns first appeared in 1941 and continued regularly for the next 38 years

In years past, there was nothing more memorable for a young boy than riding a pony on his birthday. Edward Armfield Jr. would certainly have seconded that opinion on September 9, 1949.

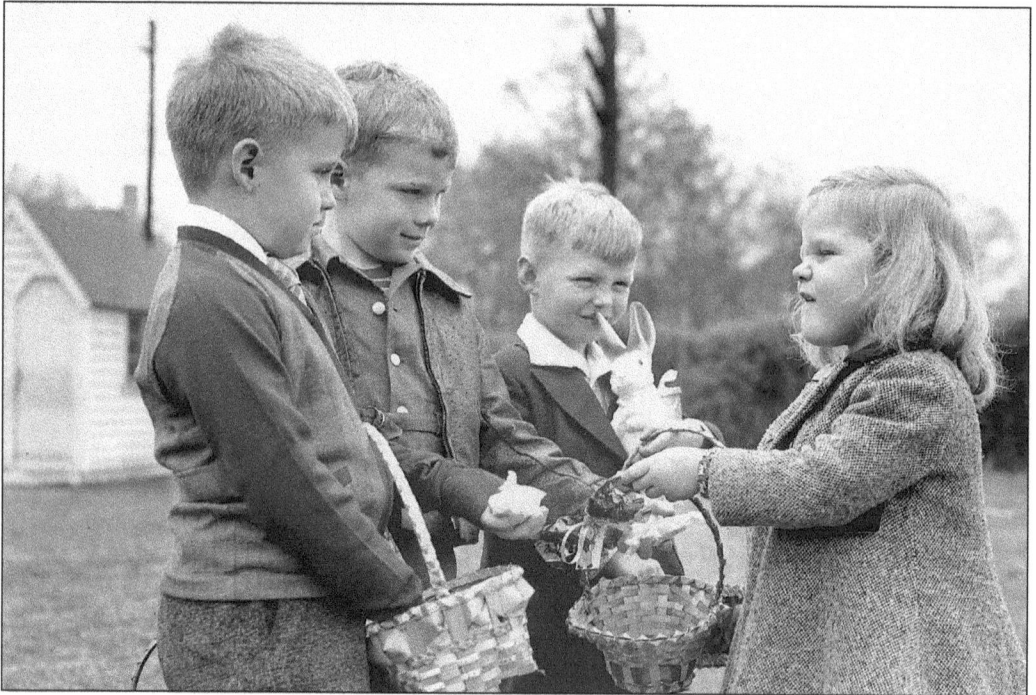

Published in the *Greensboro Record* on April 8, 1939, as part of an Easter feature, this image shows some "negotiations" over the spoils of the hunt. From left to right are Billy Rivers, Tommy Darst, Brandon Drinkard, and Jennie Lou Wyrick.

"Can we help you Larry? Please! Please!" Mrs. Pinyan's kindergarten class on Price Street was the setting for Larry Marsh's third birthday on November 24, 1948.

This small band performed at the WBIG studio on March 26, 1947. They may have been part of the WBIG's "Junior Radio Club" or "Kiddie Cabaret," which the station hosted during the 1940s. It became so popular that they moved the show to the Carolina Theater, where it eventually became the "Circle K. Club" radio program that many people still remember.

"What are you supposed to do at a birthday party anyway?" was the question of the day when

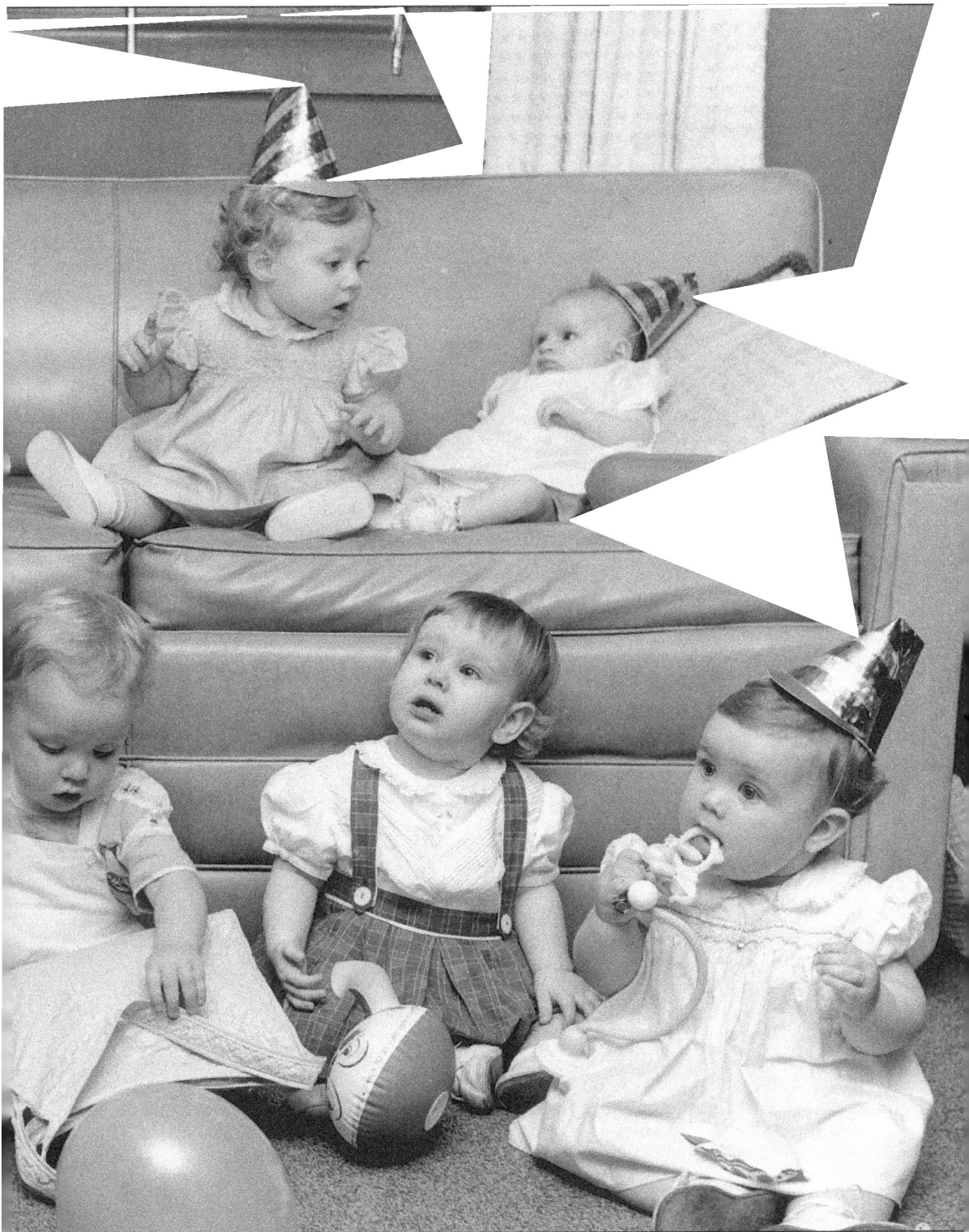

Mrs. Charles Schoolfield's child turned one on December 7, 1951.

"What time is it?" "It's time to go see Howdy Doody's Clarabell the Clown over at the new Colonial Supermarket at 1724 Battleground Avenue!" these Greensboro kids might have refrained on May 8, 1952. Guest celebrity appearances have always been a big draw at openings of new stores. Of regional note, "Buffalo Bob" Smith, the host of the popular children's show Howdy Doody, was a North Carolinian and lived in Flat Rock until his death in 1998 at the age of 80.

These unidentified children are enjoying a Halloween party sometime during the 1940s. The name Halloween originated from Hallows Eve, which in medieval England came the day before All Hallows Day on November 1st. Catholic and Anglican churches glorify God for all his saints, known and unknown, on that day. Over the centuries, peculiar customs developed on the night before—mumming and masquerading, displaying jack-o'-lanterns, and ghost and witches tales—some of which apparently were pagan survivals from older Celtic celebrations.

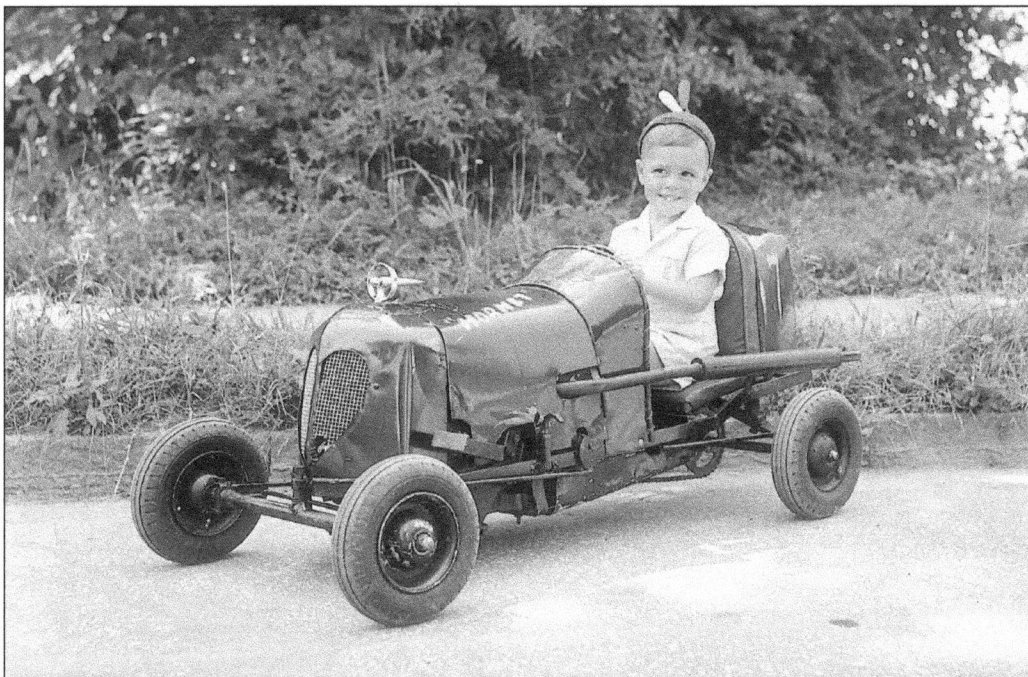

There was one obvious question to have asked Mrs. Aileen Norwood's son on August 27, 1948. Which will spin faster, your tires or your propeller cap?

These school children, like almost everyone else during WWII, did their share of collecting scrap metal for the war effort. The spare keys they brought in may have been part of the November 1942 drive when Greensboro students turned in over 311,000 pounds of scrap following President Roosevelt's August appeal. He had urged all boys and girls to "perform a great patriotic service" by collecting scrap metal, rubber and rags, and even tinfoil from chewing gum and cigarette packs.

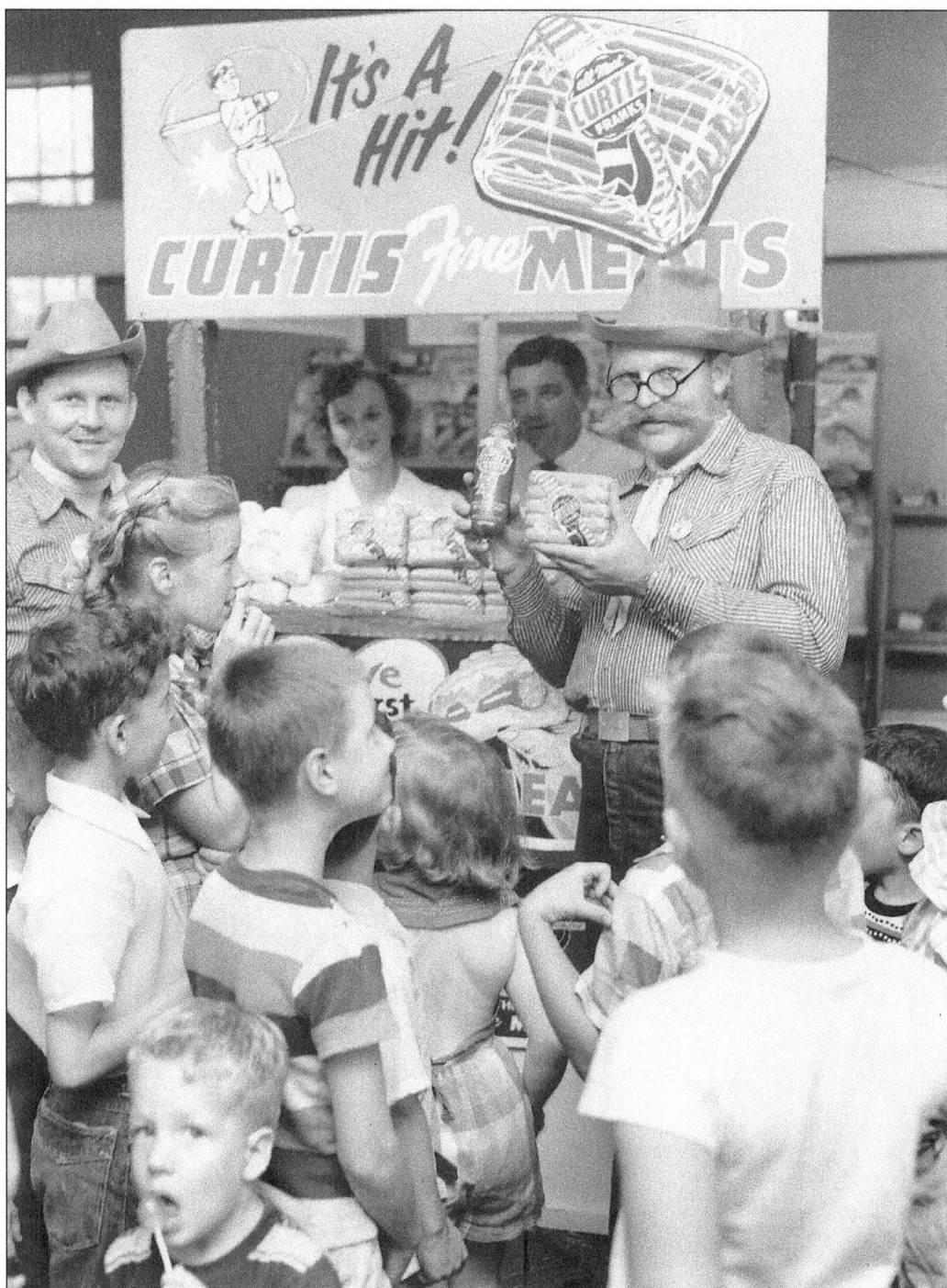

Promoting products was an essential job of Old Rebel (George Perry, right) and Pecos Pete (Jim Tucker), seen here at Ralph's Food Palace on Lawndale Drive on May 26, 1954. It was as children's entertainers, however, that each had the most lasting local impact. *The Old Rebel Show*, which was a live children's program, showcasing slapstick humor, skits, cartoons, and celebrities, ran on WFMY-TV from 1952 until 1976.

These young swimmers are getting instructions from a lifeguard at the Jefferson Country Club Lake on June 10, 1953. The lake and 92 acres of this former club were recently dedicated as the new Price Park.

Western Electric employees held their annual picnic at Country Park on August 17, 1952, where a big attraction for their children, small and not so small, was a ride on the miniature train. Later named the "Little Crescent," the chamber of commerce dedicated it to the "Youth of the Community For Better Living Through Recreation." For well over a decade, it remained just plain fun for local kids.

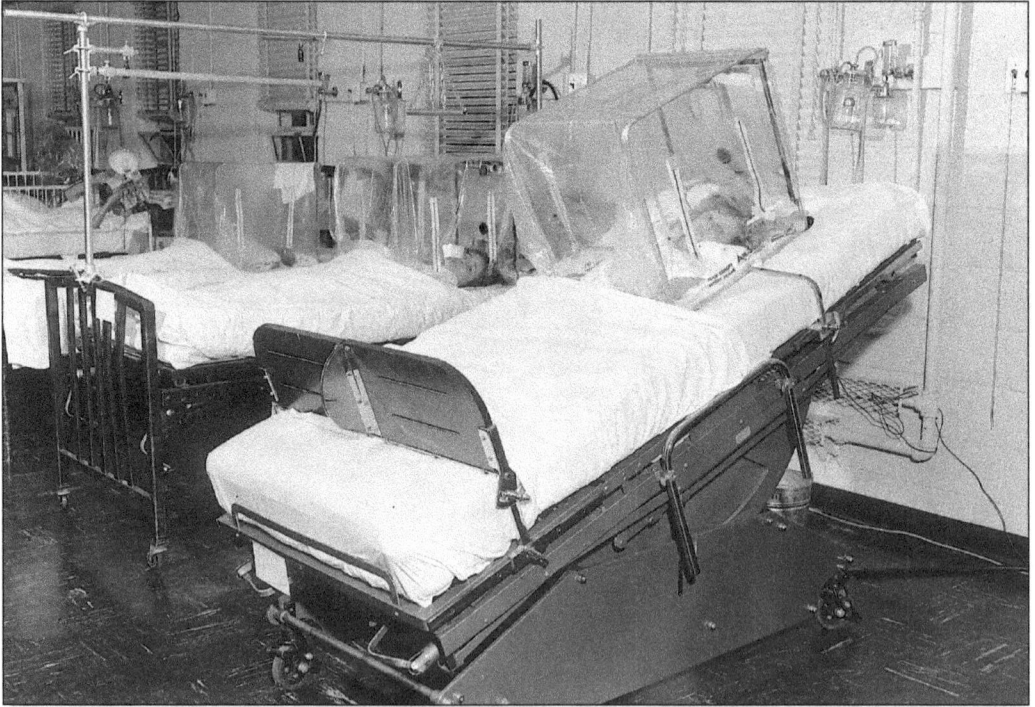

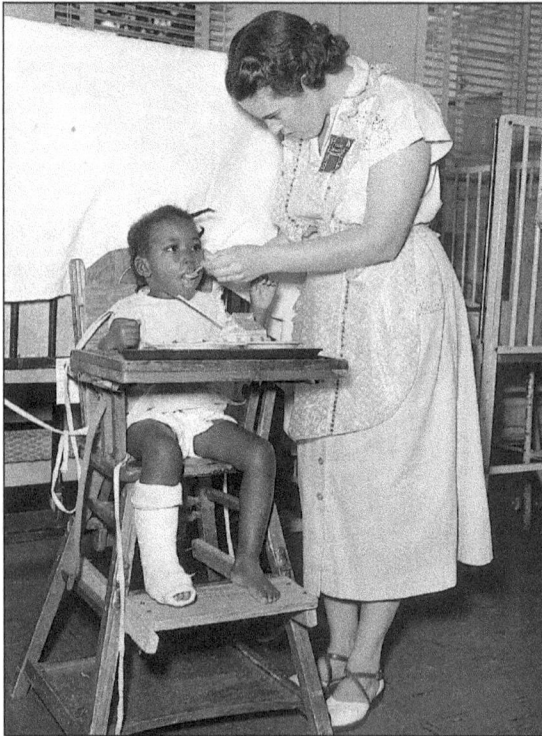

Oxygen tents were a frightening reality for families and children during the polio epidemics of 1948 and the early 1950s. In fact, the 1948 epidemic hit Guilford County more severely than any area of the country. The community responded quickly by building the Central Carolina Convalescent Hospital, seen here on March 27, 1952, in just 95 days. It took such a widespread tragedy, however—and perhaps having to look into the eyes of such young, innocent children—for the age-old custom of racial segregation to be suspended, at least temporarily, for both patients and staff.

Seven

FACES

Buildings and structures shape a city, but people define the community and give it life. Although Martin's Studio took all types of photographs, the majority of its work consisted of individual or group portraits, whether shot formally in the studio or candidly out in the field.

Here is a small sampling of the faces that breathed life into our 20th-century community. From the nationally famous, such as Louis Armstrong, Richard Petty, and Joan Crawford, to such local notables as policeman "Sunshine" Wyrick, Dr. William M. Hampton, and A.P. "Red" Routh, Martin's Studio captured their images, and as the 21st century dawns, some of the faces seen here are still with us today.

Alton P. "Red" Routh, sitting with his wife Margaret at a game on October 16, 1954, was principal of Greensboro (Grimsley) High School from 1934 until 1969 and had taught and coached there starting in 1926. On this Saturday night, the Rouths and over 9,000 spectators witnessed Greensboro High School, the reigning state champions, beat Winston-Salem Reynolds 27 to 13 to extend their record to 6-0. The game had been rescheduled from the previous night, after Hurricane Hazel dumped 12 inches of rain on Greensboro (and ended a severe water drought).

The celebrated CBS correspondent and journalist Edward R. Murrow and his wife, Janet, are seen here at the Depot on February 18, 1942. Murrow spoke to a capacity crowd at Aycock Auditorium that night about Britain and the war. The local "Janet Murrow Bundles for Britain" chapter had also been named for his wife. Murrow was a native of Guilford County, having been born on Polecat Creek on April 25, 1908. However, his family soon moved to Washington State in 1913.

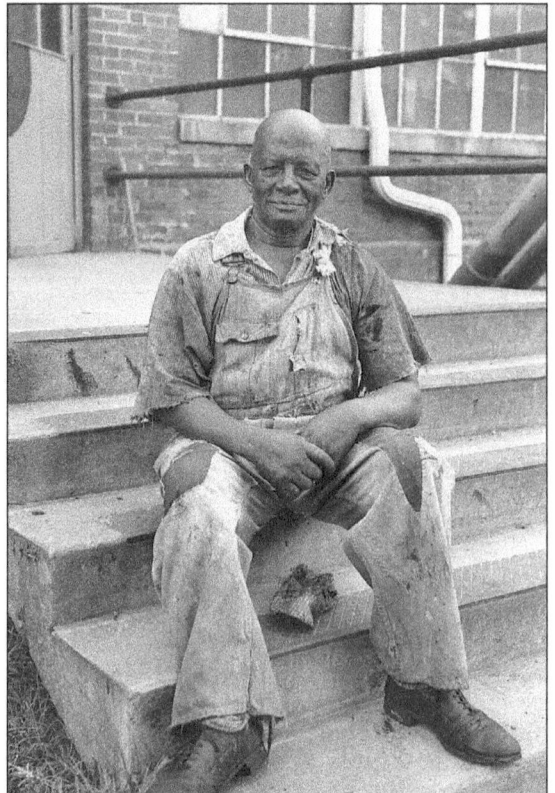

Mr. Silas Wadlington worked in the dye room at Cone's Proximity Mill when this image was made on August 18, 1946.

Martin's portrait of Richard Petty was made for Ray's Restaurant at the studio on November 8, 1971. Petty, from nearby Level Cross, won $115 in his first race in 1958 and was voted Rookie of the Year in 1959. He eventually won 200 of the 1,185 NASCAR races he entered, including 55 super speedway victories and 7 Winston Cup Championships, and he would earn close to $8 million in total winnings. Petty received the Medal of Freedom, the highest U.S. civilian award, in 1992.

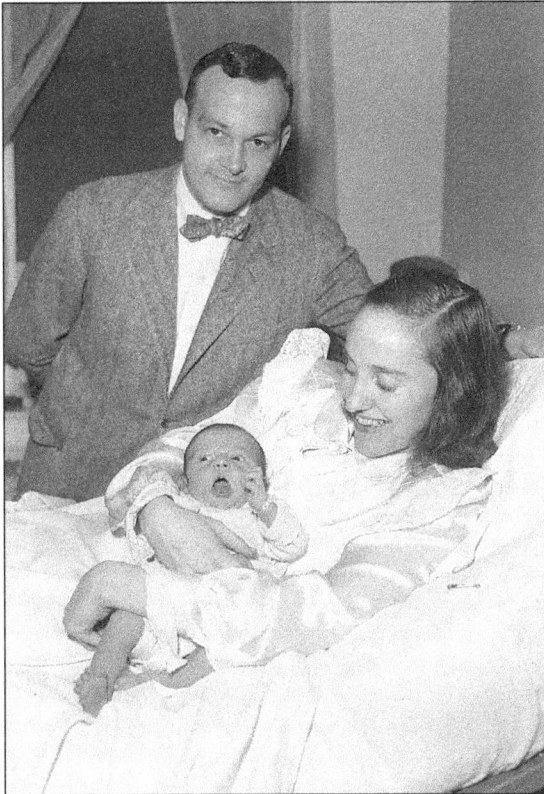

Lawyer (future judge, future congressman) L. Richardson Preyer and his wife, Emily, proudly pose with their new son, L. Richardson Jr. on March 5, 1948, in Sternberger Hospital on Summit Avenue. Young Junior seems to be talking into an imaginary portable phone, and you can almost hear him saying to his parents, "In less than 40 years, two business friends and I are going to create Vanguard Cellular Systems in Durham, and then sell the company to AT&T in 1998 for $1.5 billion!" How accurate young Preyer was.

Jim Melvin posed for this photograph at the Sedgefield Country Club on March 15, 1963. Melvin was the general chairman of the Greater Greensboro Open, which was won that year by Doug Sanders; he collected $5,500 of the total purse of $37,500. Melvin went on to become a city councilman, was elected as mayor by the council in 1971, and then became the first popularly elected mayor in the city's modern era in 1973.

William Lonnie Revels Sr. sat for Martin's on August 3, 1972. A native of Robeson County and a graduate of Wake Forest University, Revels moved to Greensboro in the 1960s and helped found the Guilford Native American Foundation in 1975. He served on the Greensboro City Council as the first Native American member from 1983 until 1987. In 1985, he was appointed by Governor Martin as chairman of the North Carolina Commission of Indian Affairs.

Dr. William Milford Hampton posed in his office on May 19, 1951. Hampton came to Greensboro as a physician in 1939 and soon became involved deeply in all levels of community service. "I feel that every man owes a debt to his community and city," he said, "and that to pay this debt he must not take everything out of it without paying some of it back." Such commitment and integrity led to Hampton's election as the first black member of the city council in 1951, and he was re-elected in 1953. At a time in which all council seats were filled by at-large citywide vote, and not by districts, this was a significant historical achievement.

Actress Joan Crawford (born Lucille Fay LeSueur) was at the height of her popularity when she came to Greensboro on May 2, 1957, to help open the new Pepsi-Cola bottling plant on Spring Garden Street. This was no paid appearance, however, since her fourth husband, Alfred N. Steele, was then chairman of the board of Pepsi.

81

Dr. Isaac H. Miller Jr., president of Bennett College, sat for Martin's on July 23, 1971. Dr. Miller, whose father had been a dean at Bennett College in the 1920s, became president of the college in 1966 and served for 21 years. During his tenure, he is credited with improving the curriculum and overseeing a capital fund campaign to endow scholarships and chairs and promote faculty development. He also helped raise funds for a new health center and promoted the development of an active alumni association.

Poet Robert Lowell was captured in a contemplative moment at Woman's College on March 25, 1945. He was visiting the college a year before winning the 1946 Pulitzer Prize for his poetry in *Lord Weary's Castle*. Lowell mastered traditional poetry and then later, with his 1959 *Life Studies*, came to be credited as the father of such "confessional" poets as Sylvia Plath, Anne Sexton, and John Berryman.

Mrs. Philip Allred's son struck an angelic pose on November 26, 1957.

When Martin's made this image on May 1, 1961, Joseph S. Koury's career as the most significant real estate developer in Greensboro's history had yet to be realized. Koury was born in Burlington in 1925 and started a small textile mill there in 1946. It was his Guilford County partnership with Bill Kirkman in 1952, Kirkman & Koury, that created a real estate empire. The pair constructed over 8,000 homes in 20 years and, in 1961, began commercial construction. The result, before Koury's death in 1998, was Holiday Inn Four Seasons, Four Seasons Town Centre, Joseph S. Koury Convention Center, and the Grandover Resort & Conference Center.

Actor Ronald Reagan is seen at a General Electric Company (GE) meeting at the Sedgefield Inn on March 17, 1955. He became a spokesman for GE in 1952—the same year he married Nancy Davis—and toured the country to give promotional and inspirational speeches. His then latest film, *Tennessee's Partner* with Rhonda Fleming and John Payne, opened the year before and his next one in 1957, *Hellcats of the Navy*, brought he and Nancy together on the screen for the first time.

Local businessman John L. Vines, posing at his business on September 9, 1958, was inventive in more than just his dry cleaning profession. He and his wife, Rose, helped create the African-American United Service Organizations (USO) club during WWII. Located on the top floor of his building at East Market and Dudley in 1944, the club helped to secure his reputation as the "Father" of Greensboro's black USO.

Charles V. "Sunshine" Wyrick (an uncle of "Moon" below) was a fixture at the Elm and Market intersection during the 1930s and early 1940s. He became a policeman in 1921 and before long was well known because of his highly visible post, which, in the era before interstate highways, brought all traffic through the middle of town. Traveling locals often mailed picture postcards back home addressed only to "Sunshine, Greensboro, N.C." with no doubts that the mailman knew where to find the recipient.

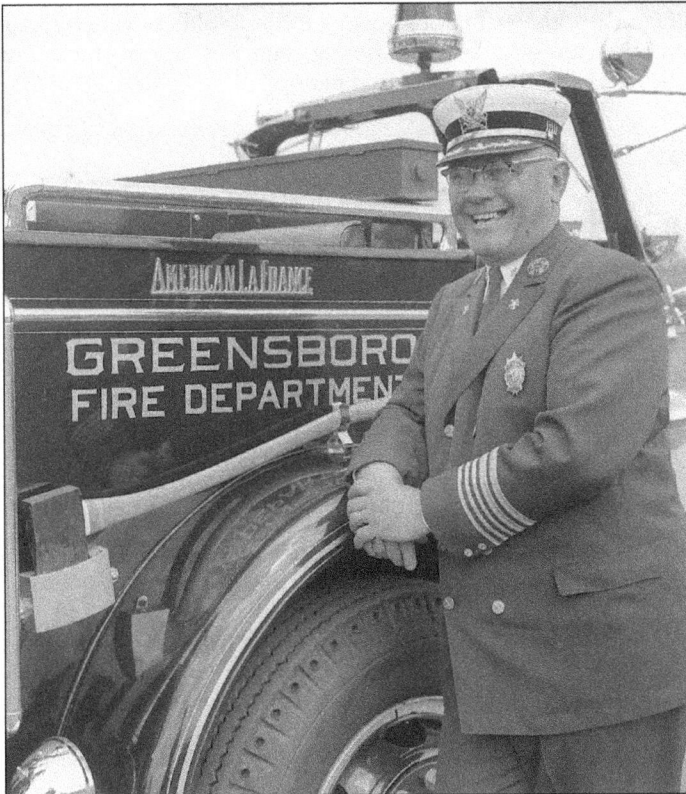

Calvin W. "Moon" Wyrick was a 20-year veteran, and only 40 years old, when he became chief of the fire department in 1946, a position he held until retirement in 1969. Under his colorful leadership, the department grew from 5 stations and 98 firemen to over 190 firemen and 11 stations. During his reign, the first 28 African-American firefighters were brought onto the force in 1961; women "firemen" were not added until the 1970s. Moon's nickname was earned early in his career because of all the "half moon"-shaped fruit pies he brought to lunch. He is also still remembered for the nearly 40 years he played Santa Claus in the city's Christmas parade.

85

First Lady Eleanor Roosevelt, seen here with Gov. J. Melville Broughton on March 31, 1941, visited North Carolina several times during the 1940s, both before and after Pearl Harbor. North Carolina contributed significantly to the war effort—over 2 million soldiers were trained in the numerous bases throughout the state—so keeping morale high was one of the many important wartime duties that politicians and their wives often performed.

Mrs. Mary Seymour sat for Martin's on January 12, 1978. She was well known in the community as a member of numerous local boards, organizations, and commissions. Seymour served on the city council (1967–1975), became mayor pro tem (1973–1975), and represented Guilford County in Raleigh as a state representative (1977–1986) as well as a senator (1987–1994).

When Sandra Hughes came to Martin's Studio on May 16, 1974, she had been working at WFMY-TV for two years. She graduated from North Carolina A&T State University and has worked at this station ever since. In her numerous broadcasting roles at WYMY TV—general assignment reporter, host of "Sandra & Friends," co-host of PM Magazine, manager of Community Affairs, and anchor of News 2 at Six and Eleven—Hughes has become a visible and respected resource and voice of the community.

Estelle Lawson Page was the most dominant woman golfer in the Carolinas during the 1930s and 1940s. In the era before a professional woman's tour, Page was considered one of the best female golfers in the world. She won the 1937 national championship, as well as seven North and South Amateur titles prior to 1945.

Herbert Hazelman, seen here in an undated photograph, came to Greensboro (Grimsley) High School in 1936 and quickly reestablished the music program, which had been suspended because of the educational cuts brought on by the Great Depression. Hazelman became a legendary teacher, musician, and mentor to hundreds of students until his retirement in 1978. Among his many accomplishments is his 1949 musical composition of the school's Alma Mater.

Dr. George Harrison Evans came to Martin's on September 28, 1948. After obtaining his medical degree from Meharry Medical College and serving his residency at the Polyclinic Hospital in New York City, Evans began practicing medicine in Greensboro in 1935. He was on the medical staff at L. Richardson Hospital until his general retirement in 1981. Dr. Evans was very much involved in the wider community. He served a crucial role as chairman of the Mayor's Committee on Human Relations during the civil rights demonstrations in 1960 and served an equally important role for ten years as a member of the Greensboro Board of Education. He received the NAACP's Man of the Year award in 1981.

These women are getting up-to-date information in a pre-natal clinic held at L. Richardson Memorial Hospital on May 19, 1948. Between 1940 and 1950, Guilford County's population increased by more than 37,000, with African-American citizens totaling about 20 percent. This period of relative growth and prosperity still saw high infant mortality rates at 27.8 deaths per 1,000 live births, which translated into 126 infant deaths. Although very high, Guilford's 1948 rate was comparable to other counties at the time, but unfortunately, Guilford has had some of the higher statewide infant mortality rates in more recent years.

Louis Armstrong posed with local WCOG disc jockey Al Troxler on February 14, 1957. Armstrong, in town for a concert the next night at A&T College, was an internationally known celebrity by the 1950s. Although always the consummate entertainer, he used his celebrity platform in the heated political climate later that year when he spoke out against the school integration confrontation and violence in Little Rock, Arkansas. A year before his death in 1971, Armstrong summed up his philosophy of life in the following statement: "All I'm saying is, see what a wonderful world it would be if only we would give it a chance. Love, baby, love. That's the secret. Yeah."

This image of local radio celebrity Dusty Dunn was taken on February 17, 1978, when Dunn was working for WBIG. Dunn has had a lengthy career over the airwaves and is still going strong. He moved recently from WSJS radio in Winston-Salem to the new WWBG station in Greensboro. Its 1470 AM frequency is the same spot on the dial that WBIG occupied until it went off the air in 1986.

Eight

SPORTS

Carol Martin, and later Malcolm Miller, captured many magic moments in local and regional sports: Choo Choo Justice around end, the Rose Bowl game at Duke, Slamming Sammy Snead winning the first GGO in 1938, Arnie's Army in 1967, stock car and motorcycle races at the fairgrounds, to name just a few.

When Martin came to the *Greensboro Daily News* in 1938, he found a good outlet for his personal interest in sports with plenty of local and regional action to keep him busy. It was not easy work, however, for sports photographers of that era were challenged by the heavy Speed Graphic and Graflex cameras and sometimes even by the lack of supplies. During WWII, Martin often went to a game with only four or five sheets of 4-x-5-inch film. Although we do not know what plays or action he may have missed in the early years, the surviving images demonstrate that his eyes, reflexes, and anticipation were equal to the challenges he faced.

The National Association for Stock Car Auto Racing (NASCAR) was founded only two months before this April 18, 1948 race at the Greensboro Fairgrounds (the Coliseum parking lot today). Some 10,000 fans witnessed a disputed race that Sunday afternoon when Red Byron of Atlanta was declared the winner over national points leader Fonty Flock. It was soon determined, however, that the 30-lap race had actually gone 31 laps and that Flock was ahead on the final lap. Byron did not let that get him down since he went on to win the 1948 NASCAR Championship.

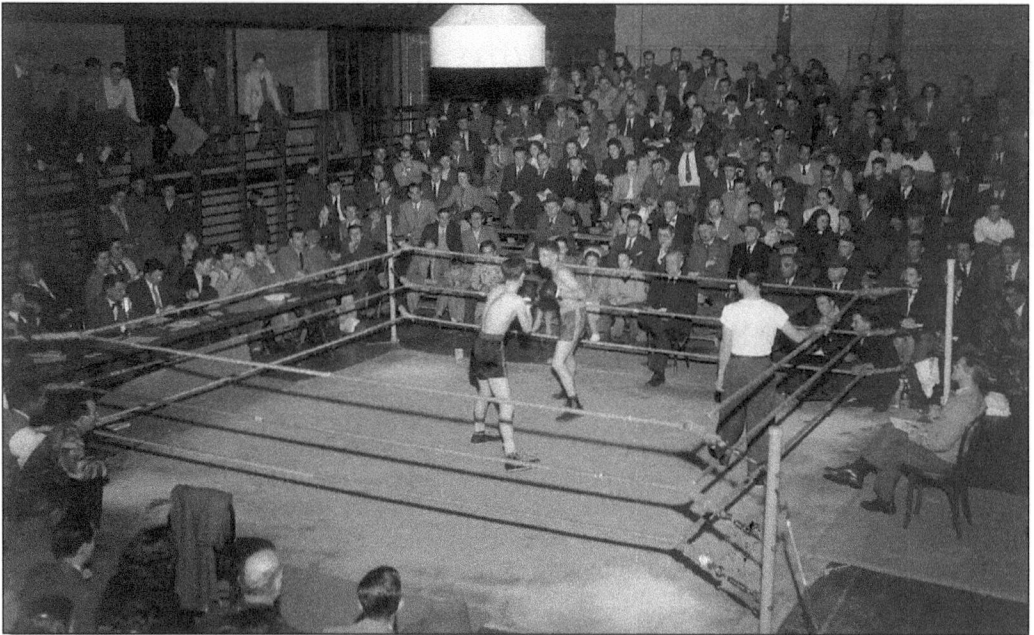

A capacity crowd came out to watch the Golden Glove tournament at the Market Street YMCA on March 1, 1947. Featured in the open division were military boxers from the 82nd Airborne Division versus Marines from Cherry Point. The FlyBoys won five of the eight matches that night.

Sam Snead, seen here at the first Greater Greensboro Open at Starmount Country Club in 1938, won a total of eight GGO titles: 1938, 1946, 1949–1950, 1955–1956, 1960, and 1965. His 27-year span between his first and last title is still a PGA record. In all, "Slamming Sammy" won 185 tournaments in his long career, including three Masters, three PGA Championship titles, and one British Open crown. An interesting bit of trivia is the fact that of the 37 holes-in-one during his career, Snead used every club in his bag to knock them in except his putter!

92

Gene Sarazen, who played in the 1940 and 1942 GGO, was the inventor of the sand wedge iron, which he first used to good effect when he won the 1932 British Open. The "Squire," who always played in knickers, won seven major championships and was the first player to win all four Grand Slam titles (U.S. Open, British Open, Masters, and PGA Championship).

Ben Hogan played in five GGO tournaments from 1938 to 1942, including this one in 1940. His 1940 total score of 270 was worth $1,200. Hogan, from Dublin, Texas, is considered one of golf's legends, not only for his numerous victories—he won the British Open, U.S. Open (four times), and Masters (four times)—but also for a gritty, indomitable spirit. He was paralyzed in a 1949 automobile accident, his doctor's advising that he might never even walk again, but he refused to quit, and in 1950, he won the U.S. Open. The Ben Hogan award is given annually to a golfer who has successfully recovered from injury to compete again.

Byron Nelson blasts out of a trap at Sedgefield's 18th green in 1941. He shot a record 64 in the second round that day and went on to win the tournament with a score of 271. Nelson competed at the GGO from 1939 until his final event in 1945, which he also won. The victory in 1945 was part of an amazing string of 11 straight PGA tournament wins.

Arnold Palmer gathered a lot of attention from his "Army" at the 1967 GGO. Palmer, who went to school at Wake Forest, became the first Atlantic Coast Conference golf champion in 1954. After turning professional, he soon developed a devoted gallery of admirers and is credited with helping to elevate the sport to new levels of popular appeal. Palmer came in third at the 1967 GGO, and he never won the tournament in Greensboro. His closest, most agonizing finish came in 1972 when, as many of his fans painfully remember, he had a two-shot lead on the final day, then triple bogeyed the 16th at Sedgefield to lose the tournament to George Archer.

94

Crowds were packing the track at the July 1946 Soap Box Derby races in Winston-Salem, as local racers competed for the chance to compete at Derby Downs in Akron, Ohio. The national Soap Box Derby races, which first began in 1934, were suspended during WWII, so this was the first post-war competition. Sometimes known as the world's greatest gravity race, the goals of the competition have always been to teach young adults the skills of workmanship, perseverance, and the spirit of competition.

Charlie Weston and Wayne Sudderth head out on a hunt with their dogs on November 1, 1952. By the time this image was taken, hunting had become more of a sport than a livelihood or necessity for most North Carolinians. The growing urbanization of the state also brought on more bureaucracy and regulation for hunters after 1927, when the North Carolina State Game Commission was created and took over the licensing procedures from the Audubon Society.

Greensboro (Grimsley) High School played Durham to a 6-6 tie in the 1938 state championship game in Chapel Hill. The solid uniforms belonged to GHS, and pictured, from left to right, are #18 Warren Johnson, #36 Herman Smith, and #30 Ray Sawyer. GHS won state championships in 1942 and 1954, tied in 1956, and won its last state crown in 1960.

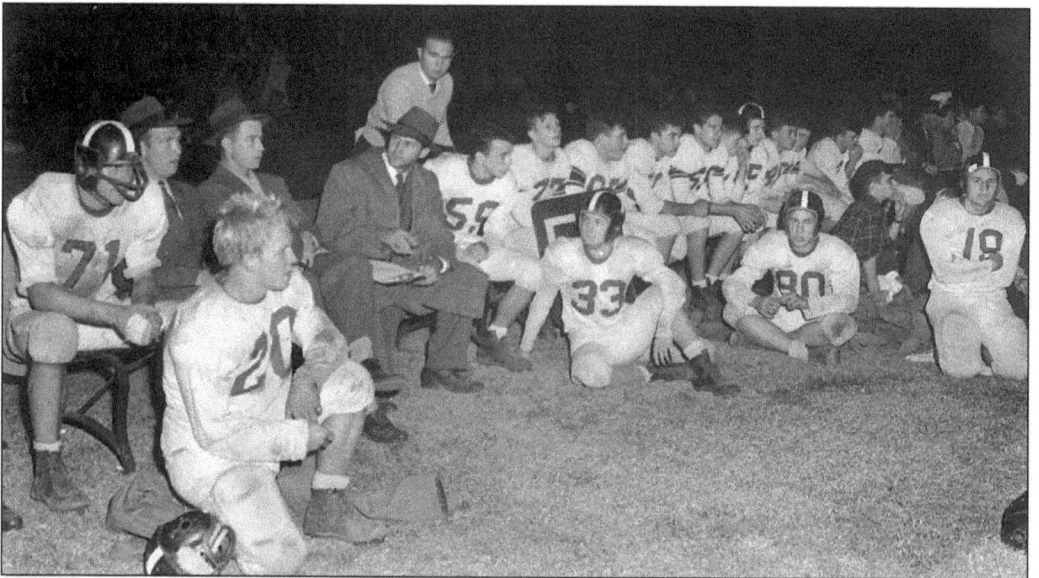

Coach Bob Jamieson (in hat at center) is seen with his team at Memorial Stadium around 1946. Greensboro (Grimsley) High played their games at Memorial until the campus field opened in 1949. Jamieson came to Grimsley in 1933 and in the next 42 years won 17 state titles in various sports, including four state football championships (with three additional ties). Of note is the face mask worn by Joe Melvin (#71). At that time, only players who had face injuries wore them, and face masks did not become standard equipment until the 1950s.

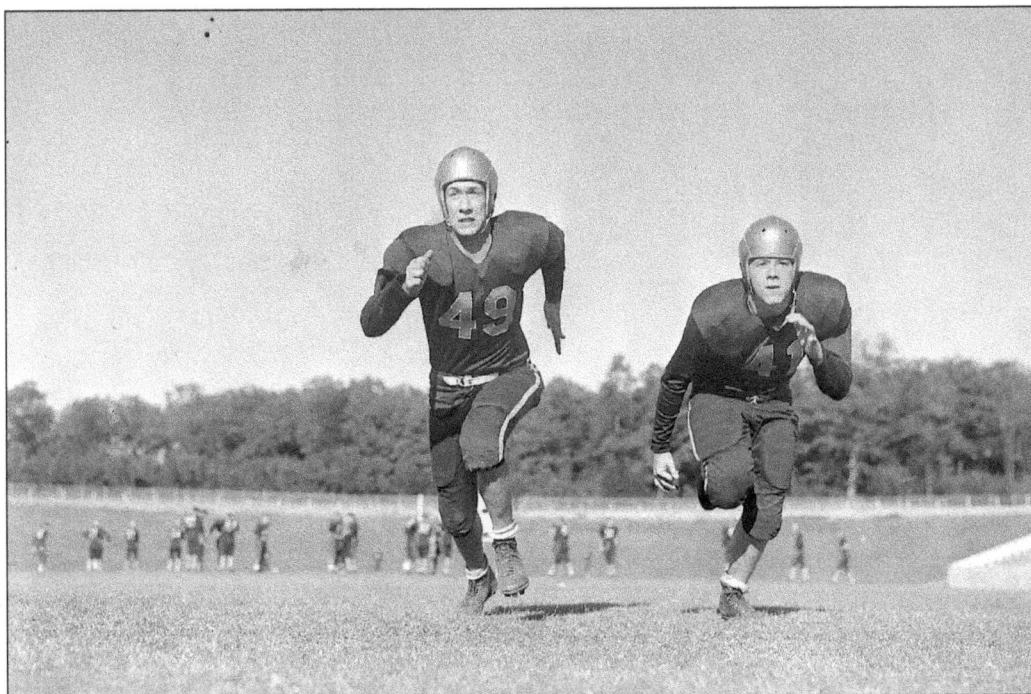

Jim Leonard (#49) and Jim Eller (#41) warmed up for the "Purple Whirlwinds"—as Greensboro (Grimsley) High was then known—before playing Reidsville to a 7-7 draw on October 21, 1949. Some 4,000 spectators saw a GHS team that was still considered one of the state's football powerhouses.

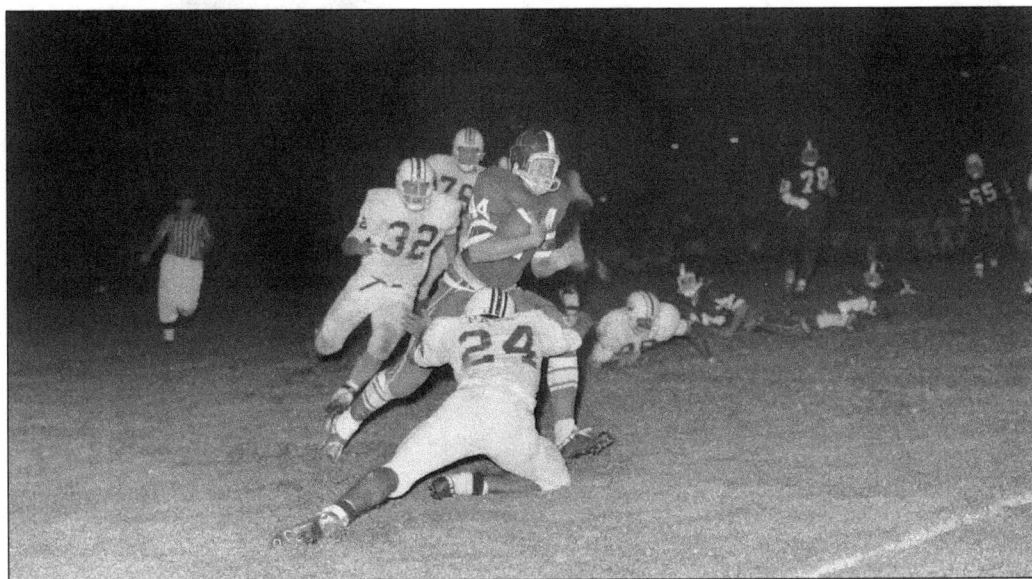

The Page (in white) versus Grimsley game on October 13, 1967, has a familiar ring to it. Grimsley leads Page 7 to 0 going into the second half, but late penalties cost Grimsley an excellent scoring opportunity, and they lose 7 to 12. Grimsley did not beat Page in a regular season game from 1971 until 1999, when a 27-14 victory on October 15th finally ended the streak.

UNC's Charlie "Choo Choo" Justice, seen here following Cotton Sutherland's block in a game against Wake Forest at Chapel Hill in 1946, was a multi-talented runner, passer, punter, and kick returner. He came out of Asheville Edwards High School and military service ball to lead Coach Carl Snavely's single-wing attack to a 32-6-2 record from 1946 to 1949. Not only was

Justice a consensus All-American, he finished second in the Heisman Trophy balloting in both his junior and senior years. Interestingly, he still holds two state high school rushing records: 18.6 yards per attempt (in 1942), and his career average of 14 yards per attempt.

It snowed for the entire game in Durham in 1938, which should have favored the northerners from the University of Pittsburgh. But in the third quarter, as this rare Martin image shows, Duke's Willard "Bolo" Purdue blocked Pitt's end-zone punt. Duke recovered and went on to win 7-0, which gave them a perfect season of 9 and 0. This put Wallace Wade's "Iron Duke" team, which outscored its opponents 114 to 0 that year, in the Rose Bowl against the University of Southern California. Duke's perfect season ended with a heartbreaking loss on January 2nd, when Cal scored in the final minute to win 7 to 3.

The Rose Bowl game between Duke (dark jerseys, with stripes) and Oregon State on January 1, 1942, moved to the East Coast following the December 7th attack by the Japanese on Pearl Harbor. Although large gatherings were banned on the West Coast, the stadium at Duke—yet to be named after its then-current coach, Wallace Wade—was packed that day. Duke had another 9-0 record going into the game but lost 16-20. And thus, for the second time in three years, Wade and Duke came up empty-handed in the nation's premier amateur sporting event.

UNC tries to gain yardage against State College (North Carolina State) at Kenan Field in their 1947 game. Although the Tar Heels won 41 to 6, which was a common occurrence during the Charlie Justice era at Carolina, State had come into that season with great confidence. Under Coach Beattie Feathers, the Wolfpack went 8-2 the year before, which had earned them their first bowl invitation. They lost 34-13 in the Gator Bowl to powerful Oklahoma.

This 1938 Southern Conference Tournament semifinal game, played at Memorial Auditorium in Raleigh, is one of the earliest sports images Martin took for the Greensboro papers. Duke defeated Maryland 35-32 in this game and went on to beat Clemson 40-30 in the finals. There were over 11 teams in the Southern Conference then, prior to its break-up and the resulting formation of the Atlantic Coast Conference. That historic event happened in 1953 at the Sedgefield Inn in Greensboro. In 1954, the conference chose Greensboro as the site of its offices, at the old King Cotton Hotel, and it has remained in town ever since.

Curry High School hosted Winston-Salem at their gym on Spring Garden Street on January 13, 1961. Curry usually had enough players for basketball teams, but its small student body (never more than around 300 students) had problems fielding a full football squad. Under legendary Coach Herbert Park, however, Curry won several state six-man football championships.

The Page High Pirates were unbeaten in conference play when they went to Grimsley the night of January 10, 1967, but lost 40 to 52 to their cross-town rivals.

Amateur and professional baseball was the major national sport by mid-century, as this crowd at a semi-pro baseball tournament game at Memorial Stadium in 1938 suggests. The stadium, which opened in November 1926, has been host to all types of events over the years, both professional and amateur, sports and non-sports. During WWII, Wednesday evening was "Fight Night" at the BTC#10-ORD military base, and at dusk, over 10,000 soldiers would march down Summit Avenue to the stadium, singing traditional Air Force songs, ready for the pugilism to begin.

The All-American Girls Professional Baseball League played a game at Memorial Stadium in the 1940s. The league operated from 1943 to 1954, with the Kenosha Comets (Delores Brumfield White, left) and the South Bend Blue Sox (Mary "Bonnie" Baker, right) as two of the original four teams. Baker was an all-star catcher for South Bend until 1950 and, later, the only woman manager in the league. The women's league began by playing, in essence, underhand-delivery, fast-pitch softball, using a 3-3/4-inch diameter ball, with the mound 40 feet away. By the league's last year, however, they were using a regulation size baseball (2-3/4-inch diameter) and throwing overhand from a mound 60 feet from home plate.

John Richmond, Maceo Wadlington, and Matthew Richmond were softball players on the East White Oak veterans team of July 1946 and also a part of a recreation wave that rose up after the years of hardship caused by the Great Depression and WWII. With much more leisure time and an obvious commitment to enjoying it, sports such as softball grew in popularity. Slow-pitch softball, in particular, became a recreational favorite because it gave batters a better chance at hitting the ball than did fast-pitch or baseball.

The "hounds" follow a horse and rider over the fence during the Sedgefield Hunt in 1941.

Nine

ENTERTAINMENT AND LEISURE

After WWII, Americans worked hard but also played hard. The growing prevalence of 40-hour work weeks and fatter pay checks left more leisure and entertainment time and opportunities for the average American.

Carol Martin and Martin's Studio caught a lot of our local pastimes on film. Whether it was dancing to Benny Goodman's band at the Sports Arena, roller skating at the rink on West Lee Street, lining up at the National Theater on South Elm for a live performance by Eddie Arnold, taking in a movie at the Palace Theater on East Market, lounging on the beach and dock at Hamilton Lakes, or dancing to big-name bands and performers at the Casa Blanca or Plantation Supper Club, many of our leisure activities were captured by a Martin or Miller lens. We are lucky that while we were playing and relaxing, they were working hard to preserve the moment.

Benny Goodman and his band played at the Sports Arena on September 16, 1949. Prior to the Coliseum and Memorial Auditorium opening in 1959, many popular musicians performed at this East Wendover arena, which was a converted WWII Overseas Replacement Depot recreation building. Admission was $2 that night for the "9pm-till?" performance of the "King of Swing."

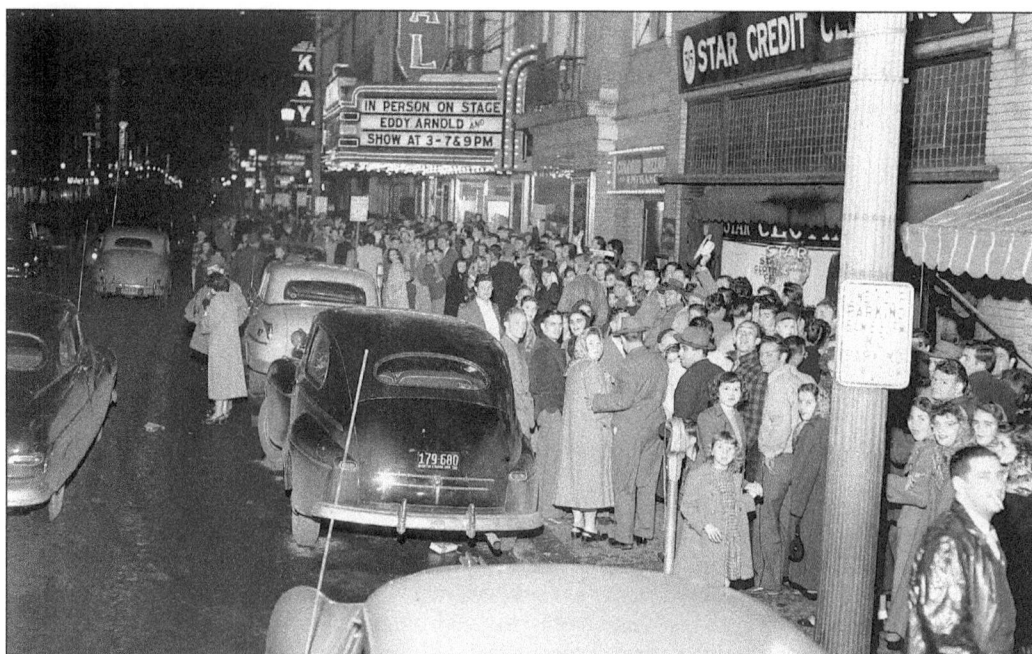

The long lines outside the National Theatre at 311 S. Elm on January 30, 1950, were there to see singing sensation Eddy Arnold (below). The National, which opened in 1921, also showed first-run movies and frequently generated big crowds, which was also the case when Elvis Presley appeared in 1956. The theater closed in 1966, and the building was later razed.

Eddy Arnold, considered one of greatest country/pop singers of all time, was reaching his full stride of success when he came to Greensboro on January 30, 1950. It cost 74¢ to see "The Tennessee Plowboy & His Guitar" in one of his three shows. Arnold had four number-one country music hits in 1949, including "Show Me the Way to Your Heart" and "Don't Rob Another Man's Castle," and 1950 would bring "Take Me in Your Arms and Hold Me." Incredibly, Arnold has had hits in six decades, has sold over 85 million records and CDs, and unlike his big 1965 hit "Make The World Go Away," he never has.

This local gospel group, the Victorious Glorylanders, played mostly in this area but did tour the country some during the 1960s. From left to right are as follows: (seated) Frank Thompson and Ezel Maness; (back row) James Pennix, Gilbert Snipes, James Watkins (manager), and Alfred Smith. All were from Greensboro except Thompson, who was from High Point. Alfred Smith later joined the gospel group the Keystones and toured throughout the nation and world.

After the Beatles hit the United States in 1964, teenage musical "combos" became very popular. This unidentified band is playing at Archie Kottler's bar mitzvah on March 25, 1967.

The Rebels, which included the soon-to-be-well-known Billy "Crash" Craddock (seated, at left), played Fred Koury's Plantation Supper Club in May 1957. The Koury newspaper advertisement read, "These boys are returning after a most successful tour of clubs and TV in Detroit and points North. They are really on their way to the top."

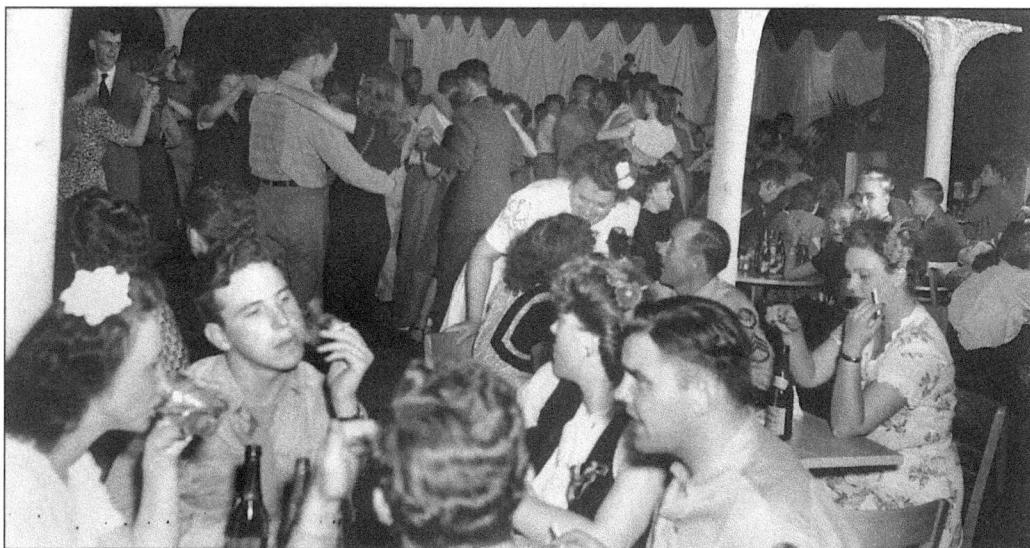

The Casa Blanca Night Club, seen here on opening night in October 1945, was located at 2700 High Point Road. It operated for seven years and was a popular club, especially for servicemen from the Overseas Replacement Depot in Greensboro. The Casa Blanca closed by 1953 and was taken over a year later by the Moose Club and later still by the Tropicana Supper Club.

This was the night—September 22, 1949, at 8 p.m.—when evenings in Greensboro changed forever. The crowds at Emile Hodge Appliances at 220 W. Market are watching, with great curiosity, WFMY-TV's first night of full programming. After running a test pattern the prior 30 days, the 22nd brought an evening of programs: "Introducing WFMY-TV," followed by a five-minute newscast, a 10-minute local film, a 15-minute musical show, and the CBS *Arthur Godfrey Show* and *College Football Thrills*.

The new TV programming demanded the hardware to view it, which is what these potential buyers were checking out at Southern Appliance on October 3, 1949. Like the early automobile industry, there were many companies producing television sets in the early years, particularly after the floodgates of consumerism opened following WWII. The Capehart brand was named for the inventor and innovator Homer E. Capehart who, besides later becoming a three-term Republican senator from Indiana, is best know for helping to orchestrate the extremely successful comeback of the Wurlitzer jukebox company after its near collapse during the Depression.

Clarence Tucker took this image of these pint-size skaters at the rink on West Lee Street on March 12, 1949.

110

Martin's made this image on March 4, 1948, at the Greensboro Roller Rink at 1413 West Lee Street. The rink was a popular place both for leisure and club skaters. "Boots" Roberts Snead (middle) and her sister, Ruth Roberts (right), were serious competitors who trained there for major national meets. The Snead family (Boots, Dennis, Dennis Jr., Jack, and Charles) went on to win numerous national and international awards and competitions. Pictured on the left is Miss Joann Purcell.

Pitching horseshoes was a relaxing lunchtime diversion on April 10, 1951, for these workers at the Vick's Plant on Milton Street.

The Greensboro Poultry bowling team is posing beside the then-popular duck pins and small balls at the Greensboro Bowling Alley on N. Elm Street in September 1950. This alley was one of two then operating in town. It had been there since the 1920s but was closed by long-time manager Paul Cox in 1959, when the lease expired, and a larger alley was built at Friendly Shopping Center. Bowling has been one of the most popular participatory sports in America over the last 100 years. After the Women's National Bowling Association was formed in 1917, it became a major recreation for middle-class women.

Definitely not on "the hot seat," these girls are getting a little extra cooling from blocks of ice on a hot July day in 1949, at the Oakhurst Swimming Pool off High Point Road.

The lake at the Jefferson Country Club, seen here on July 4, 1951, was an oasis of relaxation for 73 years. Until the club closed in 1997, employees of Jefferson Standard (now Jefferson-Pilot) Life Insurance Company enjoyed recreation and leisure activities at this suburban retreat off New Garden Road. This piece of property, far in the country when Julian Price purchased it in the 1920s, became prime real estate in the last decade. After Jefferson-Pilot decided to sell the land, controversy over its development erupted between developers and preservationists. On June 13, 1999, 92-two acres of the property were dedicated as Price Park.

Martin captured these boys "Knuckling Down" in a game of marbles sometime during the 194(
Unbeknownst to them, they were playing an extremely ancient sport. Terms such as aggie
glassie, mib, and slag are rooted in 16th-century England and more contemporary Americar

street language. A verse from the 1771 poem "Marbles" suggests that little has changed: "Knuckle down to your taw / Aim well, shoot away / Keeping out of the Ring / You'll soon learn to Play."

The Palace Theater, located at 905 E. Market Street and seen here on August 11, 1946, was one of seven movie houses in town during the 1940s. It was the principal African-American theater in Greensboro prior to integration, although the balconies at the Carolina and National were open to African Americans during these years.

There were two Zesto locations in Greensboro from about 1951 to 1958. Henry C. Liles managed this one in Irving Park at 1405 Sunset Drive, seen here on September 5, 1950, and the other location was at 239 E. Market Street. Zesto ice cream is still sold today in certain parts of the country.

These outside and inside views of Honey's Drive-In at 3000 High Point Road were taken on March 20, 1963. Honey's was a popular fast food drive-in that operated at this location (the present-day Olive Garden) from August 1961 until the mid-1970s. Y.L. Honey of Charlotte was president of this chain, which opened a second location in Greensboro on Summit Avenue in 1970.

This outdoor grill on display in May 1953, at the Home Service Store at ORD suggests at least one question. Were outdoor grills a female invention? Would moving the cooking apparatus to the back yard, where the primordial male instinct and his love for roaring fires (How about some gasoline to fire up the grill!), overcome the deadly "man in the kitchen" label? If so, it was a clever invention indeed.

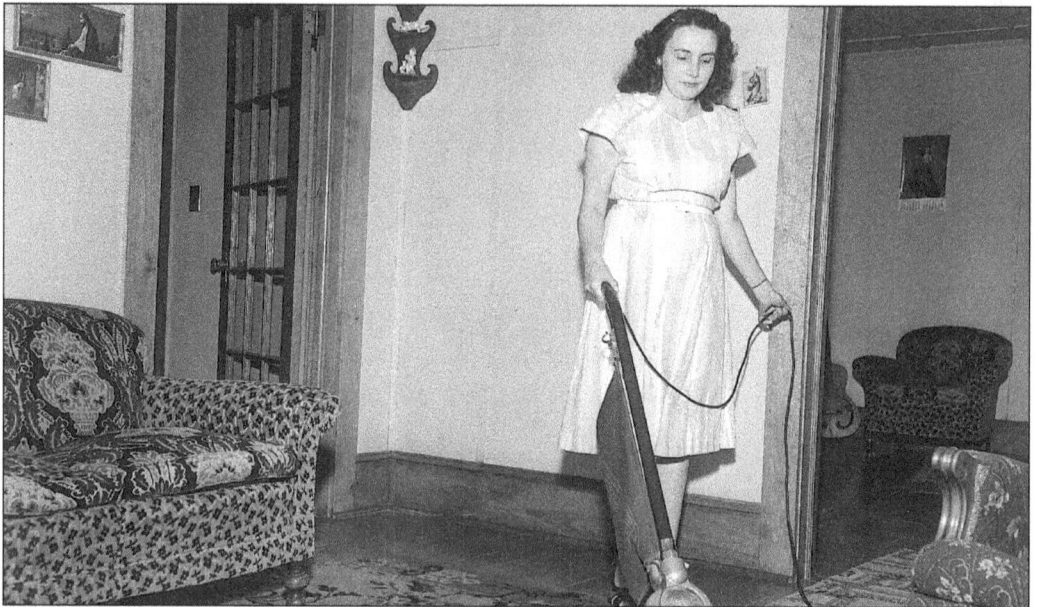

The "Leisure" category might not be the best one for this image of a Burlington Mills employee in her Lexington, North Carolina, home on September 2, 1948. In theory, however, mechanical and electronic conveniences were to have brought mankind, or womankind, much more leisure time. Historians of technology and culture still debate this idea, however, with questions like the following: when it becomes so much easier to clean, do we then come to expect cleaner houses so that we end up spending as much or more time cleaning the house than we did before?

118

Ten

BUSINESS AND INDUSTRY

Business and industrial accounts are some of the most profitable for professional photographers. During much of Martin's history, local businesses and industries did not have their own in-house photographers. If companies needed portraits of their employees or images of their products or services to include in a report or publication, they called on a commercial photographer.

From its beginning in 1947, Martin's Studio documented all aspects of the business and industrial community in Greensboro, whether it was white-collar workers at Jefferson Standard or blue-collar jobs in factories or service industries. Carol Martin tended to stay in the studio more, making portraits and taking care of day-to-day business, so Malcolm Miller did a majority of the industrial and business photography. This led to an interesting identity crisis for Malcolm, who would sometimes be greeted on the streets with a "Hello Mr. Martin."

Osbey Smith and his wife, Elizabeth, managed the Jonesboro Grocery Store at 1909 East Market Street when this image was made around 1946. It was one of the numerous businesses in the thriving African-American community on East Market. Five of the 21 African-American grocery stores in town were located on this street.

Belk's Department Store was bustling with Christmas shoppers on November 26, 1954. Belk's, at the corner of Elm and East Market, was not the first local store to get escalators (Meyer's Department Store was the first in 1949), but they were still an interesting novelty in 1950s Greensboro, 50 years after having made their first appearance at the Paris Exhibition of 1900.

This May 11, 1954 spring fashion show, held at the Belk's Department Store, was a big "haute couture" event for Greensboro.

John Crawford and Grover Dean owned the Half Moon Cafeteria when this photograph was made on September 21, 1948. The 1948 City Directory lists a total of 121 restaurants but only 18 served a "colored" clientele. Competing cafes on East Market included the Casbah (at 935), Red Lantern (at 921), and the Royal Garden (at 821). When the Half Moon closed, around 1961, there were 155 restaurants listed, and although still segregated, the custom of designating "colored" restaurants in the city directory had ended.

"What Stanley products would you ladies like to buy today?" Selling to housewives at home during the day, in this case at H.S. Covington's on Westridge Road on September 15, 1952, was a common occurrence after WWII and before women began to enter the workplace in greater numbers in the 1960s. Founded in 1931, Stanley Home Products is still in business today as a division of the Fuller Brush Company.

The new 1949 Fords drew the curious to Ingram Motors at 315 N. Elm Street in 1948. There was tremendous pent-up buyer demand after WWII. New car production had ended in February 1942, and when it began again in mid-1945, the automobile industry entered a boom period. Greensboro automobile registrations alone jumped from 12,167 in 1947 to 14,325 in 1948.

City Motors and its Rambler dealership opened at 238 N. Eugene in October 1959. American Motors Co., which was founded in 1954, introduced the amazingly popular Rambler American compact automobile the year before, ending the long history of the Nash and Hudson nameplates. By 1960, Rambler was in third place in industry sales nationwide. Such success caused City Motors to open an enlarged dealership on Battleground Avenue in the early 1970s, although their used car lot stayed downtown for several years.

One can almost smell the menthol and eucalyptus aroma surrounding these packers at the Vick's plant on Milton Street. When this image was taken on June 28, 1951, the Milton Street plant had been in operation for 41 years. Lunsford Richardson organized the business in 1905 as the Vick's Family Remedies Company and renamed it the Vick Chemical Company in 1911. After 1907, they started concentrating on Vick's Salve, which was renamed VapoRub in 1912. It was the great flu epidemic of 1918 that saw sales go from 5 million to 17 million jars by 1919.

The Vick Chemical Company laboratory is seen here on February 28, 1951. By the 1950s, Vick's had 18 manufactories worldwide, but its plants on Milton Street and Wendover Avenue were still producing VapoRub and other popular cold remedies. By the 1950s, the company was beginning to diversify into general pharmaceuticals, veterinarian drugs, and men's and women's toiletries. In 1981, the company became Richardson-Vicks Inc. and is now a division of Procter & Gamble.

Home delivery of milk and dairy products, seen here in Starmount on April 14, 1949, was an everyday and popular service for Greensboro residents well into the 1960s. Guilford Dairy, which was bought out by the Mayberry Corporation in 1979, was actually a co-operative business. In 1931, regional dairy farmers formed the Guilford Dairy Co-operative Association, Inc. to help farmers get fairer prices for their products. Their first plant was on West Lee Street, but then on April 26, 1949 (below), the public got a chance to tour the new plant on West Market Street, which is still in use today by Flav-O-Rich.

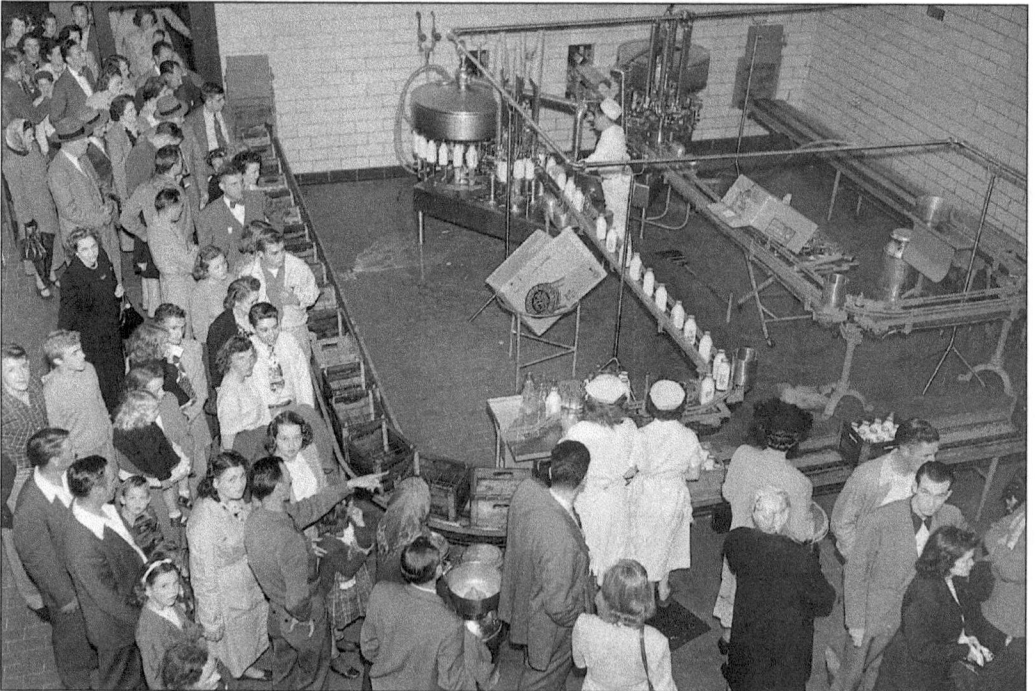

Workers stay busy at Lane's Laundry at 814 W. Market Street on October 22, 1946. Lane's, which is still in business at this location today, joined four other laundries in town when it began operation in the early 1920s. At that time, most cleaning was still done with water and soap, but the new process of "dry cleaning," using chemical solvents instead of water, was offered by all. During WWII, Lane's was taken over for military use when the Army Air Force opened a basic training center camp in Greensboro.

By March 27, 1956, most local users were only getting a Southern Bell telephone operator's voice when having to make long distance calls, and on September 25th, long distance meant all the way to Europe when the transatlantic cable began operations. Phone ownership had tripled in the prior 20 years; in October 1956, the 50,000th Greensboro phone was installed at the Richard Bernard house at 105 Kimberly Drive. Although most telephones still came in "basic black," colored models were sold as early as 1954. It was with the introduction late in the decade of the "Princess" phone, which came with a lighted dial in five colors, that telephones moved beyond mere function to stylish accessories.

The Mock-Judson plant on Howard Street was a hum of activity on March 11, 1939. The plant began producing silk hosiery in 1926 but, after 1940, "Mojud" began fashioning nylon hosiery and soon became one of the top worldwide makers of women's full-fashioned hosiery. By the 1950s, the company's 2,000 workers, working three shifts, were producing 19.2 million pairs of nylons per year. Kayser-Roth bought Mock-Judson in the 1950s and ceased hosiery production in 1972. The building recently fell silent when the Rolane Factory Outlet closed its operations.

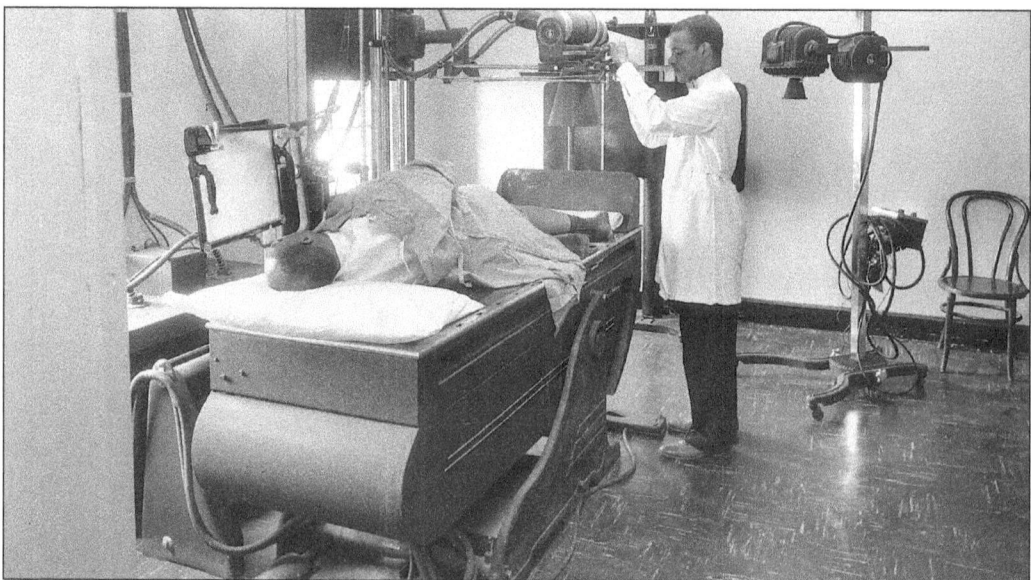

The L. Richardson Memorial Hospital x-ray room is seen here on April 29, 1953. By the mid-1950s, over 22,000 x-ray procedures were being carried out yearly, 26 years after the hospital's founding. Mrs. Emanuel Sternberger donated money for the original x-ray equipment as well as the newer machine seen here, which was part of the new addition in 1945.

Malcolm Miller took this image of the IBM Department at Jefferson Standard Life Insurance Company on January 20, 1949. These employees used machines to type or punch insurance information on to "punch cards," which could then be sorted or read mechanically by IBM machines. These were not, however, electronic computers, which came a little later. Whether mechanical or electronic, such machinery has always been vital to the insurance industry, which requires lots of data and the people necessary to produce, arrange, and analyze it. This was especially true at Jefferson Standard, which, during the 1950s, was the largest life insurance company in the South and Southwest, with over 375,000 policyholders.

Signing up for health care was a popular benefit for workers at the Sears Mail Order plant in Greensboro. By this date, August 15, 1949, The Hospital Care Association had been in existence for 16 years. The Hospital Care Association and the Hospital Saving Association merged in 1968 to form Blue Cross and Blue Shield of North Carolina, which currently has 1.8 million members.

These unknown Guilford County farmers are bringing in the fall harvest around 1943. Historically, Guilford County has always been an area of small farms, and the 1940 census confirmed this with its report that 70% of area farms (3,936) were under 49 acres in size, and only eight were greater than 700 acres. As this image suggests, most owners and workers were male. There were only 120 female farm managers or owners out of a total of 3,826, and, in 1940, the 1,080 male paid laborers had only 14 female counterparts.

As late as April 1997, when the George C. Brown & Co. plant burned to the ground, residents of west Greensboro were still lucky enough sometimes to catch the wonderful aroma of fresh cut cedar filling the air. Seen here on December 17, 1962, the Brown plant was described in the 1950s as the "largest producers of aromatic red cedar in the world." The three-year-old Greensboro Coliseum (back left) was certainly the youngster on the block when this image was made, since George C. Brown had been at this location since 1914.

www.ingramcontent.com/pod-product-compliance
Lightning Source LLC
Chambersburg PA
CBHW080902100426
42812CB00007B/2123